Cut the tape early!

The reflections of a businessman who became the go-to "Fixer" to some of America's wealthiest real estate moguls

Based On Actual Events

Jerry R. Rosen

Cut the Tape Early!

©2025 Jerry R. Rosen

Purple Works Press
41 Avenida Fernando Luis Ribas #449
Utuado, Puerto Rico 00641

ISBN: eBook 978-0-9974916-3-0

ISBN: paperback 978-1-7378873-9-3

First edition: February 2025

All rights reserved. No part of this book may be reproduced in any written, electronic, recording or photocopying form without written permission of the author, Jerry R. Rosen or the publisher, Purple Works Press.

Printed in the USA

Acknowledgments

I am grateful to the following individuals (family, friends, mentors, employers, and colleagues) for their love, guidance, and support, knowingly or not, who made this book possible. Maxine Rosen, Bertram H. Rosen, Helene M. Weinberger, Harry Rosen, Herman Frankel, Ted Taps, Arthur E. Orlean, E. Robert (Bob) Miller, The Robert A. McNeil Company, Equity Residential Company, Sam Zell, Oxford Management Company, Lyle Rosenzweig, Jeanne Hendricks, Thomas Bozzuto, Rabbi Richard Birnholz, Clifford Hardy, Related Capital Company, Stephen M. Ross, Diana Mayes, Denise Kiley, Centerline Capital Company, Marsha Jackson, and David Repka.

Contents

Acknowledgments 3
Prologue 7

PART 1 - THE EARLY YEARS
Childhood Memories 11
Moving Into a New Home 17
My Big Adventure 21
Never Underestimate the Imagination of a Bored Kid 23
Vacations In Florida 27
Vacation In Michigan 29
Vacation Across the Country 31
Losing Mom Too Soon 35
Taking My Life Back During High School 39

PART 2 - BASIC TRAINING
Working With My Father At Roth Jewelry 43
The Formal Education That Followed 47

PART 3 - PLANTING SEEDS
The Start of a Career 51
A Second Chance in My New Career 55
I Called the Number 59
Life Picked Up Speed 61
Getting Engaged, Married, And Growing Up More 63
Three Lessons Learned on a Honeymoon 67
Creating Balance, Making Adjustments 69
Sometimes It's Better to Be Lucky Than Good 71

PART 4 - TIME TO HARVEST

J. Roth and Associates Was Born 75
Busy Life And Another Blessing Arrived 77
Balancing Work, Family and More Work 79
Sometimes I Had to Say No 83
New York Souvenir and a Funny Surprise 85
An Opportunity to Work with a Developer 87
What Do You Do When Your Client is a Putz? 91
Jewelry Stores, Apartments, Optometrists 95
Why I Don't Have a Business Partner 101
Real Estate Syndication Firms Need Help Too 107
Consulting Sometimes Means Shifting Gears 115
Reaping Rewards, Taking Time Off with The Family 119
The Next Decade Brought Significant Changes 121
A Kaleidoscope of Memories; Sunrise, Sunset 125
You Are Hereby Summoned 129
Trying To Keep Up with Our Grandchildren! 131
When A Close Friend Needs Help 133

PART 5 - WHAT'S NEXT?

Looking Back, Looking Forward 141
About the author 145

Prologue

Jack Roth is relaxing on the balcony of his high-rise condo in Clearwater Beach, Florida, reflecting on his past and pondering what lies ahead. Most people who know Jack believe he has led a normal and successful life, having come from a modest middle-class mid-western family who could be anyone's husband, father, uncle, or grandfather. But Jack's life has been anything than "normal." While he played it straight and got some lucky breaks along the way, Jack made some decisions during his life that took him off the road most men with his education, background and talent may not have taken, which bordered on the edge and included decisions some may consider a lot riskier and perhaps even "barely legal."

Jack's business life contains some unusual twists, which is not what is on his mind today. Jack, who is 70, gazes toward the Gulf of Mexico at the setting sun as he recalls his conversation with a good friend and real estate attorney earlier that day. Even his wife and family are not yet aware Jack is considering becoming involved as a partner in a new affordable housing opportunity. He has connections both inside the Beltway[1] and within the real estate community to perhaps place him in a lead role. All of Jack's friends and family have long assumed that Jack would certainly be thinking about retirement at this point in his life. But what follows is not about what Jack is considering to do next or what may lie ahead. It is about his past.

Having grown up in a Chicago suburb, Jack had a normal upbringing. He was not a great student, but he was smart enough to get into a good university where he obtained degrees in both accounting and law. Jack's goal was to find out where that combination would take him. His early business life was more focused on the financial side of the businesses

---

[1] The term "Beltway" refers to Interstate 495, a highway encircling Washington, D.C., and is often used metaphorically to describe the political and governmental circles within the capital. It signifies the insiders of federal politics, lobbying, and policymaking, often detached from the concerns of the general public.

he worked for, not necessarily using his legal training. Having a solid understanding of both presented him with opportunities to work with business owners who needed his talents. They wanted someone who knew how to manage money from their companies' profits that they did not want to report to the government or investors fully. As one thing led to another, Jack became a "fixer" to some of the country's largest and most prominent real estate moguls.

On the surface, Jack maintained the image of an ordinary businessman who married his first love and had a couple of bright and not-so-ordinary children who also managed to find success in their own lives. His business life required significant travel as he pursued bigger, better and more lucrative opportunities. The one thing that may be an indication of his financial success is his pride and joy, the Mercedes Benz convertible. Jack looks like an ordinary senior living out his life with his wife on the beach in Florida. But, the following story provides an inside look at the fascinating and sometimes humorous life of an anything-but-ordinary man, written in his own words.

PART 1

THE EARLY YEARS

CHAPTER 1

Childhood Memories

I came into this world as Jack Roth on a warm, cloudy June day in Oak Park, Illinois, a Chicago suburb. I am the son of Esther and Harold Roth. I already had an older brother, Bernard Harvey Roth.

Some say a person's personality is formed during the first six years of childhood. I do not know if that is true, but I can say this: my first years of childhood seem less important to me now, compared with events that influenced my life between the ages of thirteen and twenty-one. But, for now, let us go back to those early days.

My *first* memories are of being an infant while living in Oak Park. I can remember being in a crib in our bedroom, waking from a nap and needing a diaper change. A woman I didn't recognize—and definitely NOT my mother—picked me up and told me she was going to change my diaper.

I recall our house having brown siding, a narrow single driveway, a one-car garage in the rear, and what I think was the kitchen protruding from the one side of the house toward the driveway. My "much older" brother Bernard, seven years my senior, and I shared a "dormer room" upstairs, each having our own twin bed (after I was out of a crib).

Bernard had a train set spread out on the hardwood floor. I remember wanting to make the train move, so I turned the handle on the transformer, and it began running around the tracks. Unfortunately, when I was finished playing with the train set, I didn't turn it off because I didn't know how. Later that day, we smelled smoke upstairs from downstairs. We discovered I had burned out the transformer when we went upstairs to investigate. I can still remember Bernard yelling at me for having done so.

I must have seen a Superman comic book because I also wanted to fly. One day, I jumped off the front stoop (not a porch—just a small stoop, about two steps high, leading to the front door) and landed face-first, creating a huge bump on my forehead. Apparently, the go-to remedy for swelling was to press a cold butter knife against the lump. I remember causing quite a commotion. Personally, I was just disappointed I couldn't fly.

An elderly woman lived a few doors down from us in a house on the corner lot. She gave me a stick of gum, but when I unwrapped it, I accidentally dropped it and was left holding only the wrapper. Realizing my mistake, I burst into tears. The lady noticed what had happened, picked up the gum, threw both it and the wrapper away, and handed me a fresh, unwrapped stick.

I can remember one evening in the summer when my dad was not yet home from work, and we were having a major thunderstorm. I was *very* scared. My mother held me and rocked me in a chair on our screened-in back porch, telling me that the angels in heaven were bowling. I didn't know what to think. Obviously, my mother knew very little about meteorological events. Just kidding. I was scared to death and found comfort in her holding and rocking me to get me to stop crying. To this day, I hate severe storms.

Another memory from that house occurred when I apparently picked up a stone and threw it at one of the children who lived across the street. I always had a strong throwing arm and good aim. I can remember apologizing to a little boy who was bleeding from a head wound. I guess I hit that kid right in the forehead. It was just an accident.

Childhood Memories

I only have memories in one direction from my home to the left when facing it, toward "Granny Taub's" house. She was the old lady who gave me the gum and, by the way, also made me pancakes on Sunday mornings. We moved from this house when I was about three. By the way, she wasn't a relative, just a neighbor.

My daughter Sarah and I have talked about how people her age—and kids today in general—have no idea what it was really like to grow up in the 1950s and '60s.

Mangles have largely disappeared from personal use but are still used commercially by dry cleaning companies to "iron" shirts, tablecloths, and other large items. Looking back, having a mangle in our basement was quite advanced, considering that irons had existed in various forms for centuries.

One of the most fascinating parts of watching my mother use the mangle—or an iron, for that matter—was her expert use of a soda bottle with a distinctive cork top. The cork was perforated with small holes, allowing her to sprinkle water and dampen the fabric before pressing it.

We've all seen movies of Asian women spitting on clothes while ironing. Obviously, this was a much more civilized way to dampen fabric before applying heat, which helped create an almost starched and perfectly pressed garment.

But what I remember most is the smell of the fabric being heated. We had no fabric softener back then, so perhaps modern fabric softener manufacturers have tried to recapture that wonderful fresh scent of cloth being ironed—or, in our case, mangled. It sounds funny, but it worked.

Back then, clothespins came in two varieties—but how do I describe them? I guess the best way is to say they were wood, but one was a simple, smooth clip with a carved knob on the top that, when slipped over a garment hanging on a clothesline, kept it attached. The other was a far more complicated spring device you pinched to open and let go so it would close. By the way, I don't think there was a single home in the 1950s that didn't have poles in the backyard, spaced several feet apart, with thin ropes or tightly bound twine for hanging and air-drying clothes. Washing machines appeared much earlier than dryers, so drying clothes outside in the fresh air was common. Even today, this practice remains prevalent in lower-income areas where many people still can't afford dryers or the cost of running them.

Milk chutes were another story entirely and came into vogue with the home delivery of dairy products by… the milkman (dressed in white, of course). I guess it would seem insane today for young children who are accustomed to going to the store with their parents to buy fruits, vegetables, milk, and other groceries to understand that at one time all of these things came down the street on carts, drawn by a horse or pushed by men who sold their goods from house to house. My own father had such a horse and wagon. Actually, his father did, too. But when my dad was just a boy, he helped his father sell fresh fruits and vegetables from a horse-drawn cart. It was also my father's responsibility to take care of the horse. I have no first-hand knowledge of this, but I am repeating what my dad told me. All of that had long disappeared, at least almost entirely, by the time I was a small child. I can still remember some vendors coming down the street selling food items, particularly when I visited relatives in Cleveland. I suppose the ice cream man is among many cities' last remaining street vendors.

And then there was the milkman. Early on, trucks—first horse-drawn, then gas-powered—delivered milk in glass bottles rather than cardboard cartons. As I recall, they also brought sour cream and cheese.

Most homes had a small, insulated pass-through near the driveway, where the homeowner (let's be honest—the wife or mother) would leave a note once or twice a week, along with empty bottles, to place an order for more milk or other dairy products.

Each side had a door that closed with a simple snap device—nothing fancy, just a basic latch. It didn't lock.

I've never asked anyone why milkmen wore white clothes and drove white trucks. Perhaps it was to convey an image of purity or wholesomeness.

The insulated lining of the milk chute was critical to the success of this delivery system. Milk would obviously not stay fresh in the summer if it were permitted to remain very long in a compartment that was not insulated. But fresh milk did not stay there long anyway. After all, the women in those days, the "little ladies," were mostly homemakers or stay-at-home moms. I'd guess that some women worked outside the home in secretarial positions or similar jobs and couldn't use this device. That's not to say there weren't well-educated women in important roles during this time, but they likely had help at home—someone to retrieve the milk from the milk chute, wouldn't they?

What about mail delivery? The way mail is delivered today drives many of us completely crazy. Folks are lucky to have curbside delivery these days if they live in a single-family home. In the homes in which I grew up, mail was delivered by mail carriers on foot and delivered through a proper mail slot in the front door. These were usually made of brass and had flap-type covers on the outside to help keep the elements out (rain and cold).

And hairdryers. Who has not seen at least one movie with women sitting under huge bonnet hair dryers? Beauty salons still use these in certain parts of the country, but handheld dryers, of course, have become more popular due to their size, portability, and relatively inexpensive cost. There was a time when families could buy a hybrid hair dryer, which had a bonnet but was, to some degree, portable *and* could be used at home. Every one of these that I can remember was eggshell blue or pink. The top was connected to the base with metal snap devices. When opened, they could be extended over one's head. These remained popular through the 1960s. I know because, oh, here goes, I borrowed Miriam's from time to time. Stop it! I never put on any of her makeup or clothing! So, I dried my hair. At least back then, I had some!

CHAPTER 2

Moving Into a New Home

Around 1950, my parents decided to stay in Oak Park but move into a larger home. I was told this was mainly to give Bernard and me more space and privacy. However, considering that the kitchen was nearly twice the size, I suspect my mother also had a say in the decision.

The new house, a Frank Lloyd Wright design, was a step up—likely made possible by my father's thriving jewelry business in downtown Oak Park. We now lived in a more fashionable three-bedroom, two-bath home with a single driveway and a detached one-car garage in the rear.

By this time, my throwing arm had improved enough that I could toss a tennis ball clear over the house, leaving Bernard or my dad to chase it down on the other side. I also had a red wagon and an apple crate that Bernard had converted into a pretend race car. (I even have photos of myself wearing goggles, a cowboy hat, and fringed cowboy gloves while sitting in it.)

I must have driven the neighbors crazy with my favorite toy—a plastic trumpet. I would march proudly in front of the house for what must have been hours, tooting that damn thing nonstop.

Bernard wanted to teach me to play baseball, and apparently, he took it quite seriously. Baseball was a passion for Bernard, but I was too young to understand much about the game. Thankfully, I still have photos of us both in Chicago Cubs' uniforms playing together in our backyard. And I had a real baseball glove. I can remember a dirt pitcher's mound in the middle of our backyard, from which we threw at each other. Let me correct that, from which we pitched toward each other. We used the back of our house as a backstop, so if the batter missed the ball when it was pitched, the ball would stop.

A childhood female friend (as opposed to a "girlfriend") who lived down the street, Diane Fishman, made the mistake of walking behind me one day when Bernard pitched a ball for me to hit. When I swung back to hit the ball, Diane got hit in the forehead with my bat, and she needed stitches (is there a pattern developing here?). I saw her years later when we were teenagers. She had a scar over one eyebrow but told me she had forgiven me.

I liked playing with one of the boys who lived two houses from us, but I can remember his father having what we kids were told was a stroke. It left him paralyzed. I was learning things about life, including the fact that people could become sick.

Another amazing fact about this time period was I had a significant amount of freedom, certainly much more than anyone that age would have today (I was still not even in third grade). It was the "carefree 50s." We did not worry about terrorism, nor did we watch any evening news on TV and see stories about crime taking place in our neighborhoods. It was a time of trust, or I would not have been permitted to go outside and play, which I did frequently. I did some things that bring back memories of shame and embarrassment, as well as outstanding personal achievement. For example, the fact that I tried to burn down a neighbor's home was not my finest hour. I have no idea what caused me to even consider doing that. Perhaps I was already showing signs of attention deficit. I think I always needed to be mentally challenged to be happy, but I didn't learn that until much later in life.

Moving Into a New Home

Just to clarify, I never set fire to the home itself. I knew better. I believe now that I was thinking that if I began a fire in the shrubs in the yard, a fire truck would come. I failed. Adults came, including the homeowner and then my parents. Bad idea.

CHAPTER 3

My Big Adventure

Mom had to work part-time in Dad's jewelry store once in a while. When that happened, I had to go to an older lady's home who provided childcare in her home and lived just about a mile away. This lady cared for ten to fifteen children; I remember her front yard was enclosed with a chain link fence. The windows went from floor to ceiling and were "wavy," which I found scary, and just getting into a bed required help from a step stool. I could not get on or off alone and hated taking naps there! My deal with my mother was that I would go to this home and play with the other kids, but I did not want to have lunch there. And I absolutely would not nap there. It seemed all the ladies ever served were tomato soup and cheese sandwiches. So, I wanted to be picked up by Mom before lunch. I agreed to go in the morning, but Mom was to pick me up before lunch, if possible or before nap time, at the latest. That was our deal.

One day, Mom was late. The lady who ran this prison had served lunch, and we were playing out in the yard when she called us in for a nap. Oh, oh. Mom was not there, and I was not going back into the "joint." I am told I have always had a mind of my own, and this situation was simply unacceptable to me. So, I calmly opened the gate, which had been securely closed but not locked, and against the advice and calls to me by my playmates, and with a smile and a jaunt in my step, I announced I would walk home! I could not read the street signs but was looking for a big gray, two-story home on our corner. I knew to turn right (from riding in the car). I walked two more blocks and approached my home on the left. I made it! Success!!

I proudly walked into the house through the front door (we rarely locked it) and found my mom sitting on the bottom step of the stairs that led to the second floor. She was on the black phone we had on a table there. She was talking to my dad at the store. She had already called the police to look for me and was crying. "Hey," I asked, "why the sad face? I got here, didn't I?"

My mom dropped the phone, picked me up, hugged me, and then spanked me! This may explain why I sometimes do not know how to react to certain events. Should I cry or be happy? She had arrived at the caregiver's home about ten minutes late, but I was gone. The caregiver almost needed an ambulance. Oy vey, what a mess. A kid got away! Mom looked for me but didn't see me anywhere. I was walking home. That evening, we had a guilt session, and I learned how much damage I had done to her heart, so I never did that again.

CHAPTER 4

Never Underestimate the Imagination of a Bored Kid

There were a few other episodes of aberrant behavior while we lived in that house in 1953—the year I started third grade. Looking back, I suppose I was just confused about some things, bored, and perhaps jealous that my mom had to work and leave me home with someone to "watch me."

Have you ever heard someone talking about picking a lock? I had heard you could "pick a lock," so when I found some fancy plastic cocktail toothpicks in a kitchen drawer, I decided to pick the lock on our front door. I accidentally jammed a toothpick into the lock, and the damn thing broke off. Whoops. My dad needed to call a locksmith when he got home.

- STRIKE ONE -

I liked to wrestle with a big teddy bear, one that my parents gave me one year. I must have watched something violent on TV because I remember picking up a kitchen steak knife and pretending to stab the bear. That scared our once-a-week housekeeper (Susie?), who helped clean the house and "watched me" when Mom had to be at Dad's store.

Susie saw me "stabbing" the bear and ran from our living room into the kitchen. That must have made me think I should chase her, which I did. I can recall her going down the basement steps to get away from me.

OK, that was cool. But I remember waiting patiently until I was sure she had cleared the bottom step and turned a corner before tossing the knife down the stairs. The knife bounced off the basement floor. Susie yelled something like, "That does it!" I guess she called my mom at work to come home because she simply ... quit.

- STRIKE TWO -

Boredom can be dangerous at a young age. One incident stands out more vividly than any other—the time I caused actual physical damage to our home after sneaking some of my father's favorite tools from the garage and hiding them.

Looking back, I was probably screaming for attention. Well, I certainly got it. What I didn't anticipate were the consequences.

Dad worked very hard all day, every day, at the store. When repairs or improvements to the house were needed, he did those things in the evenings and on the weekends. That included plumbing and carpentry work, as well as painting.

After he finished painting the interior walls of our home, I figured they could use a finishing touch—something more artistic. So, I added my own flair with a few crayons. Not only did my drawings in the dining room not particularly please him, but he didn't find any humor in the fact I had made considerable scratches in the side of our piano with a shoehorn I found lying around. To make things worse, I had hidden his favorite tools from his workbench in the garage that same week.

- STRIKE THREE -

When Dad got home from work and saw the crayon marks on his freshly painted walls, it put him over the edge. I can remember him telling me to go upstairs to be spanked, something that rarely, if ever, occurred. Mom cried and argued like a lawyer on my behalf, pleading for mercy and another chance for me to be good. Her plea bargain was dismissed on the grounds that I needed to be taught a lesson.

So, as I lay across my bed, I received a spank on my backside. This was not an everyday event in our home, so I cried. But one of the biggest mistakes I may have ever made followed. Dad was still within hearing distance as he descended the stairs, and as my mom held me, I looked up at her, smiled, and said something stupid to her, like, "Don't worry, Mom, it tickled."

- BOOM -

Dad stopped mid-way down the steps. Mom and I heard him coming back up very slowly. My dad stood in the doorway to the room I shared with Bernard, hands on hips, looking at me. There was complete silence. Then, Dad did the unthinkable. He announced that since I had destroyed some of his valuable belongings—and spanking clearly wasn't the lesson of the day—I would have to lose something worthwhile of my own. That way, I'd learn never to take or destroy anything that belonged to someone else again.

He then picked up my favorite teddy bear—the one he and Mom had brought back from a vacation and given to me as a special gift.

Dad started toward the stairs.

Mom cried out, "Harold, not the bear! Where are you going with the bear?"

Dad went into the backyard while Mom and I watched from the window on the upstairs landing that faced the backyard. He headed toward the wire basket where we burned things we no longer wanted (that was still allowed back then).

Dad put paper at the bottom of the container and places the bear on top like Abraham puts Isaac on the altar. I saw him look up at us in the window. I was crying hysterically, as was my mother. He lit the bonfire, which became one of the biggest fires in memory for our neighbors.

I heard later that he came inside and cried, too. But I had gone to bed at that point.

- *AND THERE WAS NO STRIKE FOUR* -

I do have a couple of other strong memories of things that occurred in that home. I was young, very young, because I had on the kind of pajamas with snaps and feet. I became ill, probably from a form of the flu, and remember throwing up in bed. That was nasty. I recall thinking that was the most unpleasant thing I had ever done, and I did not want to ever do that again. And, to this day, more than 65 years later, I have not. I have never vomited again.

CHAPTER 5

Vacations In Florida

If Dad had a good year—and from what I remember, he always did—we'd drive to MiamI Beach in February for our annual vacation.

On one trip, we arrived in Miami Beach, our usual Florida getaway, without making reservations. That's crazy in February. But for some reason, Dad did it anyway.

Well, we couldn't find a vacant room anywhere.

Finally, Dad spotted someone behind the front desk of a fairly nice hotel—a man wearing a sports coat with an unusual lapel pin. I followed Dad to the desk.

The man behind the counter asked if he could help. Dad said we needed a room for a week. The man shook his head. "Sorry, we're full."

At that moment, Dad pulled out his wallet, and a card of some kind slipped out onto the desk. Without missing a beat, he placed his hand over it—his left hand, the one with his Masonic ring.

The man smiled and asked, "So, how long has it been since you've been back East?"

CUT THE TAPE EARLY!

Dad muttered something, they both laughed and out came a room key.

As we walked away, I was puzzled. "What just happened?" I asked.

Like so many times before, Dad just grinned, let out a big laugh, and threw his arm around me. "Time to get ready to learn how to swim," he said.

He was not kidding. I never learned to swim as a little kid because it was impossible to enter Lake Michigan regardless of the time of year. It was just too cold! The Florida pools had salt water in them, which could help you float. There were jellyfish in the ocean, so we decided to use the pool. I had not learned to swim before that trip, but I did when Dad literally threw me into the pool. He had to come in after me, but he taught me how to float and swim during one Florida vacation where we did not even have a room reservation!

CHAPTER 6

Vacation In Michigan

The other most important vacation of my life—though I didn't realize it at the time—was our family trip to South Haven, Michigan.

There was a small vacation resort there that had some appeal for my parents, though I suspect it was Dad who wanted to go more than Mom.

To put things in perspective, the city of South Haven is barely a dot on the map. It sits almost directly east of Chicago, across Lake Michigan—a notoriously cold lake, even in the summer. But it was an easy drive from the city.

The resort where we stayed would later become important to this story. And thanks to my wife, Miriam, I still have black-and-white photos of it, along with other family pictures. After we were married, she carefully arranged them in an album and gave it to me as a gift one year.

Looking back, the most interesting thing about the place had to be the buildings—classic Art Deco structures with distinctive rounded edges outside and curved walls inside.

I never liked hiking because I was terrified of snakes. I also refused to go out on the lake in a canoe, convinced we'd tip over. But most of all, I hated the place because of the mosquitoes. They were so enormous,

I swear I once saw one carry off a small child... well, not really. But they did eat me alive.

The only fond memory I have of that vacation is playing in a sandbox with a really sweet little girl while Dad burned something on the grill.

She was about three years younger than me, with almost-curly (but not quite) brown hair and a surprisingly calm, charming personality for someone her age. As best as I can figure, I was around seven, and she was about four.

We shared some toys in a sandbox—a shovel, a bucket, that kind of thing—until our families called us back for dinner.

It was a one-time meeting with someone I'd probably never see again.

Except for one thing.

After we got married, Miriam and I compared some facts when I saw the photos in the album she gave me as a wedding gift on our first anniversary. The pictures had originally been in one of my old albums, but Miriam had carefully arranged them into a beautiful new one.

We checked with our families. We double checked dates and circumstances. As it turns out, Miriam has a memory very much like mine, having gone to a place that looked just like the buildings in the photos, meeting a boy about three years older than herself, and playing with him in a sandbox.

Destiny is a strange thing.

CHAPTER 7

Vacation Across the Country

The vacations we took in Florida were fun and an essential part of my life, but they weren't the most exciting or meaningful trips I ever took with my family.

One other vacation stood out above the rest.

In 1959, we embarked on the longest and most extensive trip of my childhood—we drove all the way to California and back! So many incredible things happened during that journey that capturing even the highlights will be a challenge.

Our trip began by car in Chicago. Dad used a southern route to Los Angeles and a northern route from the San Francisco area to return home, with many stops along the way. Dad's strategy was to use three drivers the first day, himself, Mom and even Bernard, to get as far away as fast as possible without stopping except to eat and use restrooms. We drove directly to St. Louis and picked up the famous and all-but-gone Route 66, as there were no Interstates. We then drove to Albuquerque, New Mexico. I remember the drive, climbing from the foothills of the Rocky Mountains to a much higher elevation.

So would Bernard, as he had the wheel during this stretch. I do not remember what the argument was about, but it was scary. Maybe

Bernard was driving a bit too fast for my father because he was yelling at Bernard about his driving. Bernard abruptly pulled over and got out of the car. He said that he had enough and would walk, but he was headed back, not forward. Dad got out and said fine, we would go on without him!

If I said my mother got hysterical, that would be an understatement. I just sank into the back seat and decided to stay out of this one. Eventually, cooler heads prevailed, and Bernard got back into the car. Dad drove the entire rest of the trip, as I recall.

Some of my favorite memories from that trip include visiting the Petrified Forest, Meteor Crater, the Grand Canyon, Lake Mead, and Hoover Dam. We experienced the neon spectacle of Las Vegas, drove through the desert, and got out to stretch in 115-degree heat—though thankfully without humidity.

Reaching Los Angeles, I saw the Pacific Ocean for the first time. Then, we drove up the breathtaking Pacific Coast Highway, visited Hearst Castle, and toured the Winchester Mystery House in San Jose. Eventually, we made it to San Francisco, where we spent time on the Wharf and at Ghirardelli Square.

After that, we turned east, passing through Salt Lake City before making the final push for home. Whew! This was a trip unlike any we had ever taken—more than two weeks on the road, an adventure of a lifetime.

A couple of things happened on this trip that deserve special mention. They come close to "supernatural events," and they can be verified. While in San Francisco, we were about to get onto a cable car for a ride down one of the steep streets when Dad spotted a restaurant where he had always wanted to go. He stopped us all from getting onto the cable car and suggested we eat first. Then, he suggested that after lunch, we take the cable car. As we entered the restaurant, we heard a great deal of commotion outside. The car we almost boarded lost its grip (brakes) and crashed into an automobile at the bottom of the street. Needless to say, the meal was great, but I have no idea what we ate.

Vacation Across the Country

Thirteen year olds embarrass easily—especially when their parents strike up conversations with complete strangers, like in restaurants.

Running into people we knew on Nob Hill was cool, but Dad couldn't stop there. Somewhere else in San Francisco, he casually approached a group of women and started chatting about where they'd been, where we were headed, and who knows what else.

Dad had a "gift of gab," which I am told I have inherited. Well, these old buzzards had just come from Yellowstone National Park, and they hated it. It was a "dry summer" or something, and the geysers were not impressive or timely. Dad had reservations the next night or two nights for us to stay at the main lodge within Yellowstone, but because of what he had just heard, he decided to call ahead and cancel. Instead, we took a different route that took us about 100 miles south of Yellowstone, through some cowboy towns, and ended up staying in Salt Lake City the night we would have been in Yellowstone.

Along the way, we drove through Reno, Nevada. Suddenly, we had some problems with the car's engine (the drive through all the mountains must have taken its toll). Dad found a Chevrolet dealer and asked them to repair the car. They said they needed the car for several hours, so we found a motel room for the night. Dad then said he needed to "take care of something" and that we should all go to bed.

The next morning, we went to pick up our car at the dealership. Dad reached into his pocket for some cash to pay for the repairs, but the person at the dealership told him to put away his money. They found the problem, *and* it was covered by a warranty as the car was almost new. Well, anyone would be happy to hear that, but the smile on my dad's face is one I will never forget. He did everything except do an Irish jig. He was grinning, for heaven's sake. "Quick," he told us, "We need to go." Dad could not hold back as we drove away from the dealership and continued on our trip to Salt Lake City. He told us he expected the repairs to the car to be at least $200 (worth about $2500 today), so when he had gone out the night before, he walked to the closest casino. About an hour later, he exited with about $250, enough to cover the cost of the repairs, but he left before losing what he had just won. So, we were now $250 ahead, covering many of the costs of our trip. I had one happy dad in the car that day. Perhaps the most bizarre part of our trip was still ahead.

We pulled into Salt Lake City, checked into a motel, had dinner, watched TV, and went to bed like any other night. The next morning, we noticed something unusual at breakfast—people were arriving from Yellowstone National Park, about 100 miles to the north.

There had been a devastating earthquake overnight. Many people had been killed; many more were missing. The travelers around us looked exhausted—they hadn't slept at all. Instead, they had spent the night in their cars, waiting for daylight so they could safely drive out of the park.

Many of the roads had been damaged and were gone. The most shocking and disturbing news was about the lodge where we were scheduled to stay. It had been mostly destroyed, and people in it had been killed.

So, that was the second time that we had escaped certain physical harm, or perhaps worse, during this vacation trip. First, there was the cable car accident, and now Yellowstone. We did not say much to each other that morning. We packed and got on the road, now anxious to get home.

Special footnote: During our entire trip, particularly in higher altitudes and warmer climates, Mom had trouble breathing and coughing. Dad even stopped and purchased a car A/C unit, which was nothing more than a device he attached through a partially open window that pushed outside air into the car. Air-conditioned cars were not yet on the market as we know them today, so this was the best he could do to try and help mom breathe better. Little did we know at the time these were signs much more was wrong with her health. After our trip "out west," that issue was addressed and discussed in the following chapter.

CHAPTER 8

Losing Mom Too Soon

Strangely, even though I have a great deal of information in my memory bank about my father, I do not have the same number of memories of my mother. I have mentioned the one or two memories I have when living in Oak Park (the thunderstorm), my memories from our homes there, the time when I ran away from daycare, mom defending me, and trying to talk my dad out of destroying my teddy bear, etc. Those things I remember, as well as picnics at home, and at the homes of friends.

All of the above having been said, my mother was still the stabilizing force at home who handled the day-to-day situations, and our financial affairs. She took care of the mail and bills. She wrote the checks. Another strong memory should be mentioned about now. She was a very heavy smoker. Almost every photo I have of her in my family album shows her with a cigarette in her hand.

Looking back on our cross-country trip to California in 1959, I remember Mom coughing a lot and struggling to breathe. At the time, it seemed natural to blame the high altitudes—especially after we reached Albuquerque—for her breathing difficulties and persistent cough.

That was one of the reasons why dad stopped along our way and purchased that "sort of" air conditioner for the car, which in reality just brought in more hot, dry air. I can recall just how hot, dry, arid, and simply lifeless the desert was, too. When mom's breathing difficulties did not improve after we left the mountains, we should have realized altitude certainly was not the problem as we were in a desert, not the mountains any longer. The problem could not be "external," she had to be ill.

Nonetheless, I recall no conversation regarding this possibility on our trip. I simply remember that we went on with our vacation to California and back. While mom's condition did not change, I was not alarmed as I was obviously not aware how serious a problem she was having breathing. Nor was I aware of any conversations she may have had with my dad.

Our trip ended in August and by sometime in October or November mom must have begun seeing our family physician. I have to guess that it led to X Rays and tests. During the time leading up to December 1959 I was, in a word, clueless. Nobody ever said to me in October, or even in November, your mom is ill, seriously ill. I don't even know to this day when she and dad discovered how ill she really was. I do recall in early December mom was hospitalized. I have a very strong memory of my mother lying in a hospital bed, under a clear plastic canopy that provided oxygen, otherwise known as an oxygen tent. In those days, oxygen was not administered via nostril tubes. The plastic covered the entire bed, something I can still clearly see. It was explained to me that the oxygen was helping her breathe better, but I was still not aware of her medical condition.

In mid-December—about two weeks before what was then called Christmas break (which, depending on the region, could fall anywhere between December 23 and January 6)—I remember visiting Mom in her hospital room with my father.

Her doctors had told her that her condition was serious. I didn't know it at the time, but she had been diagnosed with lung cancer that had already spread and was considered inoperable. While my parents were aware of the prognosis, no one had yet used the word cancer in my presence.

So there I was, sitting in my mother's hospital room as she explained to my dad the plan her doctors had discussed with her. They wanted to experiment with mustard gas. That's right. In those days, there was no chemotherapy.

My dad was in shock. His only knowledge of mustard gas was its use in World War I to kill soldiers in the trenches. He was aghast. To clarify, my mother repeated herself—this time using the phrase cancer cells.

Those who know me well understand that I have always been a fighter. But hearing these words from my mother while she faced unthinkable odds, and later watching my father battle Parkinson's disease for over twenty years—refusing to give in—helped shape who I am.

My parents chose life regardless of the odds they faced. And that's why I will never quit. Not ever. Not on anything.

Actions speak louder than words. My mother's fight went beyond a promise. She demanded to be released from the hospital and go home. She told the doctors if she remained in a bed under an oxygen tent, she would grow weaker, not stronger, and be less able to fight the disease that was taking her life. Now, whether she really believed this, or she just wanted to spend some more time at home with her family, I do not know.

Over everyone's objections she won, and came home, briefly. During her home stay, mom continued to struggle with breathing, and she was in pain. I can recall her being bundled up in a chair in our living room, wrapped in blankets struggling to breathe. I remember reading to her with my arm around her, trying to comfort her, and her nodding off. I knew she was very sick. She knew she was very sick. But her coming home gave me hope that she was doing the right thing, and by fighting her disease her way she had a better chance. At some point mom had to return to the hospital because she became too weak to stay at home. Bernard had come home from college at this point as well. It was mid-January 1960.

And then, she was gone.

When we pulled out of the cemetery, I was aware my mother was just put into the ground, and I would never see her again. But, when we got home, something changed. We have all read or seen in movies or on television what occurs at funerals in New Orleans. Well, something weird was happening in my home. People were coming from the cemetery, and after washing their hands at the front door they entered and ate. And then they ate some more. There was talking, eating and more talking. Nobody seemed sad except my dad who I found in the kitchen taking a drink of whisky from a shot glass, something I had never seen him do before. He took me into a bedroom and closed the door. "Jack," he said, starting to cry, "your childhood just ended. I need you to be strong, for me." That was it. Bernard came in, and dad left the room, wiping his eyes.

CHAPTER 9

Taking My Life Back During High School

I was in eighth grade when I lost my mother in January 1960. The second half of that school year reflected my mind's dark place. Despite the efforts of several well-meaning people, starting with my own family, I could not break through the lingering depression that had taken over my life.

But just as I entered high school, something changed within me. The more I considered what had happened to me, the more I began to build a resolve to fight back and take control of my life again. For years, my teachers had expressed their personal disappointment with me because I was not meeting their expectations in school. I started looking for a way to break the bonds of negativity and fight back.

I remember Bernard coming home from college for a short visit and bringing some homework, including one subject that gave him a hard time. He left a problem on the kitchen table to go to the bathroom or take a break. When he returned, I had just completed solving the problem and gave him my notes. His face said it all. He was astonished. He knew my grades were suffering and that I was struggling to stay alive in school. But I had just solved a college-level problem. He addressed that with me on the spot in an effort to light a fire and give me hope to move on. He did not need to; I had already arrived at the decision to challenge myself in order to ensure I had the opportunity to attend college and make something of my life in honor of my mother and to prove to myself I wouldn't let her death take me with her.

I met with each of my guidance counselors and teachers, seeking advice on improving my performance in my current classes and adjusting my curriculum to build a stronger academic résumé for college. As a sophomore, I auditioned for—and was accepted into—the school's A Cappella Choir a year earlier than was typical. I could feel the momentum shifting in my favor.

As a junior, I helped write the Distinction Day play, when juniors mock seniors with a musical parody. We called our musical "East Side Story," and I played Tony. I have a photo or two of this production. But the real fun was that I was coming alive again.

As a senior, I was seeing daylight. I was old enough to drive a car (dad's), was dating, and starting to have fun. But my greatest senior moment came in the second half of my school year. I decided to try out for the senior class play. I joined the drama club and worked my tail off to break free from the last chains of my depression by forcing myself to take the stage in a play that had only seven cast members, with one male, the lead player. I went after the male lead part. As a result of my efforts, I earned 100 points based upon the following criteria: The amount of time I spent learning my part, the fact my part was considered "major," taking significant effort to learn all the dialog, the correct cockney accent, the blocking, and the all-important timing. At the conclusion of the play, and before my senior year came to a close, I was accepted into the Thespian Society based upon the previous criteria, the reviews in the newspaper, the votes from the other cast members, and of course, the director.

I am convinced that when I entered the business world after college, the effort I put into choir and acting bolstered my ego enough to convince others I had the goods to create the successful business that followed. What follows is how I achieved that stage of my life.

PART 2

BASIC TRAINING

CHAPTER 10

Working With My Father At Roth Jewelry

Dad decided it was time for me to take on a more significant role in his jewelry business the summer before my junior year- or sometime during that year. He knew I wanted to go to college and was already researching what I needed to do to make that happen. But with Mom gone, his priority was making sure that if anything ever happened to him, I'd know how to support myself.

This became a constant subject that consumed about every conversation we had, both in the store and at home. Bernard was already out of the house, had graduated from college, and accepted a job as a forensic accountant with the FBI in their Washington, DC headquarters following a brief training stint at Quantico. His idea of stability was working for the federal government, and not only was Bernard happy with his future, but so was Dad.

I knew that my earlier school years and seeming lack of motivation had Dad somewhat concerned, even though he never came right out and said that. I believe he also saw a lot of himself in me and thought he would someday be able to turn the jewelry store over to me.

CUT THE TAPE EARLY!

I had different ambitions, of course—ones that didn't include a lifelong career in retail. But we never seemed to find the time to sit down and talk about it.

Instead, my hours at the store steadily increased—after school, every weekend, and all summer. That meant starting at the bottom: sweeping, dusting, helping with inventory, and greeting customers as they walked in. But no matter how much responsibility I took on, Dad was still in charge.

He bought the merchandise to resell, kept the books, did the merchandising, marketing, and the rest of what it took to run the business. I was still in high school, but as I watched him, observed what he did, and asked questions, I began to learn the business from behind the counter and was not just a casual observer anymore.

Every day was a lesson learned from a master. Despite never finishing high school—leaving early to help put food on his family's table—he was not only street-smart but also possessed a business instinct that couldn't be taught anywhere.

I could cite dozens of examples to help explain what I mean, but that would require me to write a book covering just that one topic.

One day, when we were alone in the store with no customers, I learned something that had somehow escaped my attention. Every afternoon, sometime between 2 and 3 p.m., Dad went behind the counter, stood at the cash register, and did something unusual. He performed a function with the register and locked it so only he could open the cash drawer. After that, if anyone came into the store and purchased something, even though I had been allowed to collect the funds for a purchase and make a change, only Dad could now do that. My day behind the counter was over for the day.

One evening at home, I asked what he did behind the cash register every afternoon. Dad started to laugh and then said, "Jack, what time do we close every day?"

"At 5 p.m.," I answered.

He continued, "So, when should we close out the register and settle the cash in the drawer with the day's receipts?"

"At 5 p.m.," I responded.

"Jack, can you keep a secret because what I am about to tell you must remain between you and me. Do you understand?" he asked.

I nodded in silence.

He blurted, "I CUT THE TAPE EARLY! All of our business is cash, right? Well, all the money that comes in from sales after I cut the cash register tape for the day goes into that little metal box under the counter."

I sat still in silence. "Isn't that illegal?" I finally asked, "Why?"

"Whose money is it anyway? Mine!" he continued. "It's just an accounting adjustment—but that part is my bonus! We still have to pay bills, rent, payroll, and everything else from our only income source, right? And I do! But if we're lucky enough to make a sale later in the day, well, that money is used for other things.

"Did you think all the trips we've taken—like our vacations to Florida—came from what I earn just in the store? No. They came from my bonuses!"

My head started spinning as I sat there, digesting what I had just heard. Later in my business life, I will never forget this lesson. Sometimes, "accounting adjustments" needed to be made!

CHAPTER 11

The Formal Education That Followed

After high school graduation, Dad and I had many conversations about my desire not to return to the store, continue to work there, and/or take it over someday. He agreed to let me "go where I wanted to go and do what I wanted to do." So, after performing my own due diligence about college and with my dad's financial assistance, I chose to attend the University of Michigan. This was in spite of the fact, or perhaps because Bernie had selected to go to Michigan State. I wanted to set my own course, which was part of my new plan for my future.

I do not know if I chose a degree in accounting or if it chose me. I also do not remember why I was so driven to attend law school either, except that I do recall many of the successful businesspeople I knew or read about had gone to law school. Two things were clear, though. I had no desire to practice law, and I have no idea how I managed to get through college as easily as I did. My study habits in my earlier days were deplorable. But I found college-level courses and the challenges that came with getting through school at that point seemed almost too easy and almost fun.

CUT THE TAPE EARLY!

Every summer, while attending college and working toward my undergraduate and law degrees, I sought out and found jobs with businesses in the greater Chicago area. I was still officially living at home, but I knew that I'd want to move out and support myself by the time I graduated. That meant earning the extra money to make it happen.

The companies that hired me knew I was a full-time student, so there was no illusion on their part, or mine for that matter, that I would someday come back as a full-time employee for them. Although there was a clear understanding regarding that fact, it made it more difficult to find good companies to work for and to get paid a decent amount of money to save toward my future after I was no longer in school. On the flip side, I began to see and learn things about some of the businesses that employed me I thought needed "financial improvement." By that, I had to hold my lip from suggesting they could be making more money if, and only if, they made some "accounting adjustments." Those observations came in handy when I entered the job market for real after school.

PART 3

PLANTING SEEDS

CHAPTER 12

The Start of a Career

One of the more interesting companies I worked for while still in school was a real estate property management company called Star Management. Arthur Klein, a wealthy real estate mogul who lived in White Plains, NY, owned the company. He had a son who attended Northwestern University in Evanston, IL. I learned Art, as we all were allowed to call him, also had a daughter who wanted to attend Northwestern after high school, so when he selected a location for his company headquarters, he chose a Chicago suburb. Naturally, he could write off his visits to see his kids at school by stopping into the office every trip from New York to Chicago.

I once suggested that Star Management was an 'interesting' company. I may have overstated that. I was hired by Henry Finkel—an older man with a bit of a checkered past—at a time when he had already seen one of his businesses go under a few years earlier. Art had found him and brought him on to run the day-to-day operations in between his visits from New York. It didn't take long for me to learn that Star Management did not exactly enjoy a stellar reputation in the real estate industry.

CUT THE TAPE EARLY!

But history was made when I was offered a position as Henry's assistant, my first real job after school. I remember, as my ticket to admission so to speak, was to pass an interview with Art during one of his trips to Chicago. He zeroed in on the fact I had degrees in both accounting and law, and I would come to learn that sealed the deal for both of us. Henry had no such education, and the only person in charge of the company's books was a middle-aged woman with a beehive hairdo who always had a pencil sticking out of it.

During my first year with Star, I learned Art had Henry create advertising for his apartments that included some of the vendors from whom he purchased goods and services. He then billed them for "their fair share" to offset the cost of the ads.

As part of my job, I was tasked with reviewing the company's books and exploring more 'creative ways' to boost the bottom line. Art didn't need a lesson in 'cutting the tape early'—he was already a master of that practice, just in a different industry.

While I was not a fan of some of Star Management's other, actually many, business practices, I was earning a salary and a separate non-taxable car allowance that more than paid for the apartment I had rented in a nearby Chicago suburb. So, I was able to stay financially afloat while trying to learn how Star actually made money and not cross any lines that would put me in personal legal jeopardy.

My tenure at Star was not destined to be a lengthy and successful one. In my first and only year with the company, a lunatic tenant we were evicting threatened me because he could not pay his rent. That same person made threats against both Henry and me by first pointing a gun at us, then a rifle. While I had wanted to remain as long as possible, first to earn as much as possible to help me sustain a living on my own, I also wanted to learn how a small, local real estate management company could become so financially viable while on the surface appearing as if they had no funds with which to manage and maintain their real estate. As I came to learn, Art Klein was the true definition of a slumlord and not someone I would be able to use as a reference if I stayed as an employee too long. So, I had to find a more reputable company where I could actually learn best practices and add value at the same time.

CHAPTER 13

A Second Chance in My New Career

When I decided to leave Star Management, I did so with a clear conscience, knowing it was necessary for both my survival and my reputation. If I wanted to work with the best and the brightest in the future, I had to walk away.

As luck would have it, one of my college buddies at UM was directly related to a more prominent and more reputable real estate firm in Chicago and introduced me to them.

I convinced the two owners of a larger, more organized real estate development and management company in Chicago to hire me—along with Andrew Owens and Tony Thomas. But Andy (as he liked to be called) was concerned about how badly my association with Star Management may have tarnished me. Tony eventually talked Andy into hiring me. Tony became my immediate supervisor, but they both became mentors to me and furthered my career over the next several years.

I went to work for The Owens Company, A&M Realty and A&M Management, all owned and operated by Andrew Owens and Tony Thomas. Following my father, Tony became my second business mentor.

CUT THE TAPE EARLY!

Working for Andy and Tony came with some interesting and important dynamics. Andy served as more of a father figure within the company, as his own father had founded it after World War II. He chose to office inside the Loop in downtown Chicago, while Tony was set up as the head of operations in a suburban office.

According to Andy, this setup was intentional—to keep operations employees from experiencing his unintended interference and to minimize distractions that might come from his daily presence. In practice, it worked. When Andy did visit the suburban headquarters, his appearances were met with greater enthusiasm and carried more weight.

From the start of my time with Andy and Tony, I was thrown into the deep end—tasked with responsibilities I had never encountered before. It was genius.

The company operated several divisions under the umbrellas of the three companies I had already named. One division focused on construction, building both single- and multifamily housing. Another specialized in acquisitions, purchasing existing multifamily properties.

But perhaps the most important—once I understood its true purpose—was a third company. On the surface, it appeared to be an arm's length affiliate providing goods and services to the other divisions. In reality, it operated under exclusive contracts, ensuring those services remained in-house.

What was this? The money was made so the operating divisions of the parent company could show and share less profit with the government and with investors, while the principals of the company were making a ton of money from this arrangement. It was legal, as far as it went, and ethical ... up to a point. What was that point? About as legal and ethical as – Cutting The Tape Early!

Within six months, I was given the title of Vice President – Operations. This was done to make everyone in the company, across all divisions, have more power within the company than as an actual promotion. However, it also came in handy for my resume when I chose to

A Second Chance in My New Career

move on after believing I had learned all I could from Andy, particularly Tony. During my tenure with the company, I traveled extensively to see for myself what was going on in the field, to learn how Tony kept all the plates spinning firsthand, and it kept me from rotting away behind a desk in the office. I got to see how the sausage was made, which led to some recommendations from Tony and Andy that came back with financial rewards for me.

After only four short years, I was ready to move on and start my own consulting company, picking up even more prominent real estate firms as clients along the way. During this time, while traveling for the company, I also got a special unexpected bonus. During one of my business trips to check out one of our businesses in Ohio, I met my wife, with whom we would start and raise a family. My life was moving like a freight train; I was having the time of my life, and the best was yet to come.

CHAPTER 14

I Called the Number

Everything was going well with my job, but something was missing. I needed a personal life. Then, I remembered another friend from UM told me about someone he dated in the Cleveland area who had a sister. He had given me that person's phone number, but I left it on my dresser in my apartment. I located the note and compared the address for a Miriam Raskin to my upcoming business travels, and there it was. I would be in Cleveland for a meeting with one of my company's investors the following week. Perfect! All I had to do now was dial the number and get the date.

When I called, Miriam's mother answered. I politely asked to speak with Miriam, and she came to the phone. As I recall, this may have been a Tuesday or Wednesday evening. Miriam and I talked for several minutes, and then we decided to meet when I was in Cleveland on Friday evening the following week. I would pick her up, and we would go to dinner. We set the time when I would pick her up after my meeting. She sounded wonderful over the phone, and I felt progress had been made!

I picked her up, we had a nice dinner, talked, and then I suggested seeing a movie. Miriam did not want to let on that this was the best date she had ever been on, and no boy had ever taken her to both a real dinner restaurant and a movie on the same date. Then we went out for dessert.

The dessert part was to prevent me from having to take her home too early. I was having a really good time, and I knew she was having fun, too. When I took her home, we stayed in the back hall of her home and talked for a while. I wanted to see her again but did not want to appear too anxious, so Saturday night would not do. "But how about going bowling on Sunday afternoon?" That worked for both of us.

We did go bowling Sunday, but who kept score? I remember thinking I was having the best time of my life. I saw myself as a sophisticated man of the world, which was saying something but also a bit of a stretch. We started to date on a regular basis when I could get to Cleveland. Not long after we began dating, I opted to lower the cost of our dates because I began to "save up,"... and I remember telling Miriam that. From almost the start, we both seemed to know where this was going. And that was good.

CHAPTER 15

Life Picked Up Speed

At this point, both my business and personal life were accelerating. I was traveling more for work and making trips to Cleveland whenever I could to see Miriam.

Financially, I was doing well enough to buy a condo in a high-rise overlooking Lake Michigan. Meanwhile, Tony and Andy asked me to start hosting 'Dog and Pony' shows at our corporate office. These exclusive, invitation-only meetings brought in real estate investors eager to hear why our company was thriving. My job was to present a polished narrative—sticking to the script on increasing income, keeping expenses in check, and improving the bottom line.

However, I was never specific about how we were improving our profits. It was not lost on me. I had a brother working for the FBI, trying to catch white-collar criminals who may be "crossing the line" in terms of tactics used to make money at the expense of others.

While these presentations were directed toward investors, I started to see owners of other real estate companies from all over the country coming as well, and we always exchanged business cards. As usual, there was always the comment about whether I should ever get tired working for Tony and Andy to "look them up." I knew the day was approaching when I would want to go out on my own, and I was now being introduced to the very people I would want as clients.

To further increase my exposure to more potential outside business in the future, I joined the largest and most prestigious industry trade associations and never missed a national conference. These were not accounting or legal professional groups; they were all related to the development, acquisition, and management of multifamily housing. Combined, the dog and pony presentations and my attendance at these professional real estate conferences proved to be the basis of how I was able to create a successful startup business when I started my own consulting firm after leaving the Owens Company.

CHAPTER 16

Getting Engaged, Married, And Growing Up More

The more time I spent with Miriam, the more I realized a few things. I knew I was in love and that she felt the same way. And we were living too far apart. It was time to take the next step in our lives and make living together formal, which meant getting married.

Miriam had graduated from Kent State and was still figuring out her career path. She worked in an insurance adjuster's office but wasn't entirely happy. Our conversations soon turned to the idea of her relocating from Cleveland to Chicago—something she didn't immediately embrace with joy and excitement. It meant leaving behind her family and friends for a city that was unfamiliar to her.

But I convinced her that if we wanted to be together, this was the path we needed to take. I wanted to stay anchored in Chicago, not just because I loved the city but because its future was rich with business opportunities.

And to be honest, moving to and living in Cleveland just did not cut it for me. I considered other cities that would be new to both of us, like New York, Boston and even the West Coast, but having been born and raised in the Chicago area, I felt a great deal more comfortable. I was confident I could convert Miriam to feel the same way after she had more time there. As "The Second City," it had many of the attractions of living and working in New York, but with a slower pace and it was more conducive in terms of starting a family when that time came. It just made sense.

Following a few visits to Chicago, Miriam finally agreed to relocate, which set the stage for my asking her to marry me. I certainly knew a great jeweler, so it was time to make introductions all around and then make it formal.

I spent some personal time in Cleveland getting to know Miriam's parents, Judith and Stephen Raskin, and Miriam spent some time in Chicago getting to know my dad. When I felt we had covered the essential introductions, I took Miriam to dinner at one of Cleveland's finest restaurants and asked her to marry me. Thankfully for me, she said "Yes," and a new chapter was opened in my personal life.

Everything in my life seemed to be on a faster track now, and I knew I was entering another stage of my life that would include a wife, children, and an extended family. At some point, I knew I would need to move on to starting and operating my own real estate consulting business. It was also clear to me that I needed to keep my priorities straight while I kept more plates spinning. Fortunately for me, I had developed excellent time management skills early in my life, as well as strong organizational skills. I began to plan further out in time, so I had a better idea of where I wanted to be and when.

It was clear to me that Miriam and I needed to finalize our wedding plans to stay on track with our future—getting her moved to Chicago and stepping into the next chapter of our lives together.

I had seen friends rush into marriage without fully considering the personal adjustments required of two people at this stage, and I didn't want to make that same mistake.

With that in mind, my highest priority became our wedding.

Getting Engaged, Married, And Growing Up More

About the time we were nearing our wedding, my father called and told me he had just been diagnosed with Parkinson's Disease. Dad said he was starting to experience more difficulty doing simple things with one hand and not walking properly. The disease was progressing, as Parkinson's does, and he knew he was slowly getting worse at performing the daily tasks required to operate a business.

He figured since I was getting married, this might be the perfect time to ask me to come with him to run Roth Jewelers. We discussed it over the phone, but I was not excited about the prospect of returning to the retail business after all the hard work and plans I had made to move forward with my own real estate consulting career. I heard in his voice the need for help, which prompted a personal visit from me to the store to let him hear it again, directly from me, that what he was asking for from me was not going to happen. It was a very difficult conversation, but necessary. We ended that meeting amicably, but I still felt guilty. I had to stick to my plan, however, and move forward. I would make up for his disappointment in other ways in the coming years by making sure we spent as much time together as possible.

Our wedding day and all the festivities associated with it arrived very quickly, or so it seemed. We planned a honeymoon that was acceptable to us both, which included going to a Bermuda resort for a week, with the promise I, in particular, would not make or take any business-related calls while we were gone.

CHAPTER 17

Three Lessons Learned on a Honeymoon

The day following our wedding, we flew from Cleveland to JFK and changed planes to catch our flight to Bermuda. For some reason, I still cannot remember why we decided to carry our luggage on the airplanes. I guess I was thinking, "Why should we check the bags?" I would have been correct if this had been a business flight, and I was alone with only my bag. I also forgot how large JFK was. All of my flights to this point were domestic, and I had never been in the international terminal at JFK. Because we were flying internationally on two airlines, we had to get from one terminal to another in just under an hour. No sweat, right? When we deplaned from our first flight, I got directions to the next terminal. I could just about see it from where we were. Buses that took passengers from terminal to terminal in a loop were available for something like 25 cents per person, but they looked slow and stopped at every terminal. I feared we could miss our flight if we took a bus, and why pay 50 cents? (Would I ever consider doing this now? Of course not, but experience is the best teacher, right?)

So, Miriam and I began our trek to the next terminal, schlepping our luggage, stopping repeatedly along the way to rest and check the time. Here is some advice. Do not do this. This was one heck of a bad way to start a honeymoon or any trip. We made it to the next flight as they were preparing to close the door to the airplane, having sweated through our clothes. Yikes. Lesson One: Spend the 50 cents and take the bus. And check the damn bags!

On the flight to Bermuda, we sat in a two-seat configuration, with Miriam by the window and me in the aisle seat. In those days, everyone got lunch, even in coach. After we had eaten, Miriam got up to go to the restroom. When the flight attendant came by, I smiled and gave her our trays. Miriam returned, sat down, and asked where her lunch had gone. "You weren't finished?" I asked. The glare. Oh, oh. She had been nibbling, and I had not looked closely nor asked if she was finished when she got up. The flight was long, and she was hungry. Lesson Two: ASK before you give away your wife's food in case she has not finished.

Bermuda was colder than we expected because I had not checked any weather reports and did not know there was a cold front affecting even where we were headed. We both caught colds. Lesson Three: Know where the heck you are going, check the weather when you take a significant trip, like your honeymoon with your wife, and, as a bonus, learn these two words: "Yes, dear!"

CHAPTER 18

Creating Balance, Making Adjustments

During the first two years after getting married, my goal was to meet the challenges of spending as much time as possible with Miriam and my dad while focusing on my business plan to become self-employed.

I continued to work hard to increase my employer's financial bottom line and kept a journal of ideas I could use with my clients in the future. Being newly married provided me with added benefits I had not known about before because I rarely even dated before meeting Miriam. I loved the company when we would go exploring all that Chicago had to offer and did things I had not previously done. It is funny how you can grow up somewhere knowing there were things to do and places to go, but I did not want to go alone for some reason. Creating a partnership with Miriam became another priority for me, something I came to realize I needed to do.

Within a relatively short span of time, we learned our family of two was going to grow to three. We did not have a plan in place to address an addition to our family, so that required another adjustment or two.

CUT THE TAPE EARLY!

And, with that came the realization I had even more financial responsibility coming my way.

In quick succession, Miriam and I set plans into motion:

1. Sell the condo and move to a western Chicago suburb—somewhere more suitable for raising a family.
2. Prepare for the birth of our first child.
3. Find a way for me to part ways with Tony and Andy while keeping our relationship intact.
4. Launch my real estate consulting business, setting the stage for the next chapter of our lives.

The plan we mutually agreed upon to move forward was sound, well thought out and executed. I owe much of my success that followed to Miriam, who turned out to be not only my best friend for life but also a great business partner.

CHPATER 19

Sometimes It's Better to Be Lucky Than Good

As Miriam and I moved forward with the real estate location part of our plan, we managed to find a buyer for the condo. At about the same time, we found a beautiful home in Schaumburg, a great place to live and raise a family. I wanted to be outside the Loop[2], and try to create a suburban lifestyle for Miriam and our family, yet not be too far from O'Hare or Oak Park. Schaumburg had everything we wanted and more. We managed to sell the condo and purchase our 'forever home' almost simultaneously.

When Eric came along later in the same year we had moved, he completed the thing missing in our home and lives: our first child. And a son at that. I spent his first days holding and staring at him, wondering if he would someday want to join me in my business. But then I came to my senses, remembering that I was not thrilled at the prospect of working in my father's business, and further, what I was doing may not be a good thing to bring a child into. I found myself imagining Eric

---

[2] The Loop is the heart of downtown Chicago and serves as its central business district. It gets its name from the network of elevated train tracks that form a loop around the area. The district is bordered by Lake Street to the north, Wabash Avenue to the east, Van Buren Street to the south, and Wells Street to the west. Known as a hub of economic and cultural activity, The Loop is home to major office buildings, renowned cultural institutions, and some of Chicago's most famous landmarks.

perhaps also going to law school but actually practicing law and doing good deeds for others as a part of his practice.

After Eric was born and everything at home was stable, I felt it was time to face Andy and Tony with the fact that while I very much appreciated the opportunities they had provided to me, I needed to break the news that I wanted to "move on" into a business of my own. I rehearsed and memorized what I would say to them separately or if I had to tell them with all three of us in a room together. I tried to imagine their reactions and prepare for the best, but I also planned for what may be hard feelings. When the opportunity arose, it was with Tony first, and Andy after Tony told him the news. To my relief, they handled the news quite well and even exceeded what I had expected. Their generosity in learning I was leaving was another life lesson for me, one I would need to remember to use in the future. Then, it was time to pack up my office and prepare for yet another new chapter in my life, going out on my own into the unknown.

PART 4

TIME TO HARVEST

CHAPTER 20

J. Roth and Associates Was Born

When I was still in college, someone close to me told me that if I ever started my own business, I should make sure to indicate to anyone what the company was about in the name. That was excellent advice, and I have often passed along that advice. That said, when I began my real estate consulting business, I was intentionally vague. I didn't want to limit myself to just one type of client. Nor did I want to work exclusively with those seeking advice solely on financial matters or legal issues. At the same time, I couldn't exactly advertise that my role was helping business owners legally maximize their profits—without landing in jail--even if that required 'creative accounting methods' and a deep understanding of the law.

Creative accounting advice is a good way to put what I provided to my clients. But how does one actually define that? I recall at a cocktail party where I had to "attend or offend," I was bored beyond belief when someone I had never met walked up to me, introduced himself in a slurred way that indicated he may have already had one too many, and asked what I did for a living. I told him, "Creative accounting."

He stared at me for a few seconds, apparently trying to wrap his brain around that, and then asked, "What the hell is that?"

I saw an opening, not knowing anything about him or what he did for a living and responded, "If your credits don't equal your debits, your assets in jail!" A few more seconds passed before this man burst out laughing and, using profanity, stated that was the funniest thing he had ever heard. Really? Who is this guy?

That guy turned out to be one of the most prominent real estate moguls in the country, who apparently was known to everyone but me. He handed me his business card and told me to call him the next day to set up a meeting. He then spun around, motioned to another man I learned was his driver, and indicated it was time to go. I stood there in total disbelief when I showed his card to a friend at that same party, who subsequently told me who he was. This was going to be the start of a very beneficial business relationship.

CHAPTER 21

Busy Life And Another Blessing Arrived

During the next several months, time flew by. Looking back, I am amazed I was able to find the time to address everything that needed my attention. I was constantly prioritizing and revising my schedule to make sure I was spending enough personal time with both Miriam and Eric, Miriam's parents (we traveled to see them as it was easier for us to go to Cleveland than for them to come to Chicago), trying to find quality time with my father, and of course, making sure my brother and I did not drift apart. We had cousins on both sides of our family, but Miriam and her cousins were always much closer than I was with mine. While that was sad, in a sense, it was also a relief. I had never been very good at maintaining certain family relationships.

While growing up in the 60s, I was exposed to a multitude of events that I know influenced my life and molded my thinking as I forged ahead as an adult in the 70s. This included my need to know I was providing for my family, but I always had doubts that was enough. The business contacts I made while working with Andy and Tony and from the conferences I attended were actually getting in touch with me, asking me to work with them. That required a lot of calls and a lot of travel for meetings, followed by hours with their staff, proposals, and recommendations that turned into revenue for me with which to support my own family.

Then, just about two years after Eric was born, Miriam told me we were expecting again. Holy cow! We never spoke in detail about any kind of plan for our family other than to let nature take its course, and it had. Once again, we needed to prepare to receive another bundle of joy into our lives. Eric had been a precocious child, but on days when I may have been distracted, he was the one thing that always brought me joy. And now, Eric was going to have a sibling. That was a lot to take in.

Right on schedule, thirty-three months after Eric arrived, we received our second blessing, this time a girl. We chose Sarah as her name and made the announcements.

CHAPTER 22

Balancing Work, Family and More Work

Unlike the turmoil I experienced in the '60s, my goal in the '70s was to remain focused on the things I have already mentioned: my family and my business. I chose to avoid the changes and political unrest that were occurring in the country. To be more honest, I was too busy making sure I kept everything else that was important to me on track. That is not to say I never lost my sense of humor or did not experience some rather interesting situations that I have never forgotten.

Miriam was a wonderful stay-at-home mom and made sure both Eric and Sarah received all the attention they needed to grow and prosper during their childhood into adulthood. I say that because my business travel picked up a lot. In order to get to meetings and do what I needed to do to make a living that would support our family, nothing was off the table as to where I would go to get a required introduction.

One day I received a call from the president of a real estate subsidiary of a giant corporation that was not involved with real estate. Bruce Martin would be my next client; I just did not know it yet. He lived and worked in New York, had received my name from a mutual contact, and decided we needed to meet as soon as possible. To bring this meeting about, when Bruce called to introduce himself to me, he launched into a plan for us to meet that was neither in New York nor Chicago. He had to attend an awards dinner in Cleveland the following week and suggested that we meet at a Cleveland airport hotel on the day he would arrive to save us time and travel effort. Bruce assumed this would be acceptable and provided the time as well. I was to fly to Cleveland, go to the Sheraton at the airport, be there by 5 p.m., and let the desk clerk know I was there. There was no discussion about who was paying for my travel, just to be there. Although my young and growing consulting business was doing "OK," I didn't want to pass up what sounded like a promising opportunity, so I agreed to his terms.

On the day of our meeting, I flew to Cleveland and went directly to the Sheraton Airport Hotel. When I called his room to let him know I was in the hotel, he asked me to come to his room. Yellow flag. After entering his room and making some small talk, Bruce told me, with my bio in view on the bed, that I would be "his guy." He then proceeded to drop his pants ... so he could change clothes prior to going to his meeting and give his speech—red flag. I backed up to the door. But Bruce was a jock, and I learned later this was normal behavior for him. He told me I would be hired if I passed a meeting with his home office team that included his accountant and legal counsel. Just. Like. That. We had not discussed the scope of work, my compensation, or any other matters one might think would be necessary at a first meeting of this type.

Bruce was in a hurry to get to his meeting, give his speech, get an award, and return to New York, so our meeting took only about thirty minutes. I returned to Chicago and told Miriam about our meeting. At first, she thought I was nuts to even entertain working with this guy. But Bruce's company was not just a New York firm, they were a national company based in New York with regions in the Midwest and eastern U.S. I knew I could negotiate consulting fees that would be significant, and I would have access to someone who could open a lot of doors for me if I did well with the objectives he had for his company.

Following our meeting and one trip to New York to meet his team, Bruce and I spoke long distance several times to hammer out a consulting arrangement that would be mutually acceptable to us both. I prepared a consulting contract and sent it to Bruce by overnight delivery. A couple of days later, it arrived back, signed. I did not know it at the time, but this one decision to take a business risk that began in an airport hotel room would turn into a much more lucrative opportunity when Bruce made some other business decisions about a year later.

The moral of this story is that if two people want to do business together, they will not let the details get in the way. But if two people do not want to do business together, the details will never bring them together.

Working with Bruce turned out to be a game-changer for me in several ways. Learning to work with a completely different personality type was educational, frustrating, and yet fun. Andy and Tony were straight-laced, close-to-the-vest, serious business owners. Andy had a law degree, and Tony came from a lower, middle-class background, forcing him to think on his feet and think outside the box to survive. They were like the odd couple, but it worked.

Bruce was tall, tanned, and handsome, and he knew it. He was as charismatic as he was business savvy. Drawn to long, black Cadillac Eldorado convertibles and huge, expensive cigars, he cut a dashing figure with women, even though he was married with kids. And, in a flash, he could go from mild-mannered Bruce to fire and brimstone if things were not going his way, and then minutes later, he was the calm, gregarious Bruce who always seemed to know how to get his way with anyone who wanted to make a business deal with him. I often thought Bruce would never have an ulcer, but he certainly caused others to have them instead.

My time traveling expanded more while working with Bruce simply because of his attention to detail and the bottom line. If he suspected one of his loyal Lieutenants in a regional office was not squeezing every last dollar out of that region's operations, he sent me to audit that region's books. Often, his instincts were spot on, and I had to report back that Bruce would be better served with someone else at the helm of that region. But that was a part of our agreed-upon scope of work, and I was paid accordingly.

Bruce was also a complex person when separating business, friends, and family. He actually brought me into his private circle of close friends, made vacation condos available to my family and me, and even loaned me his Eldorado on one trip to his office when he was out of town so I would not have to pay to rent a car of my own. My travel expenses covered auto rental, so in the back of my mind, I always wondered if that was an act of generosity or was he just being cheap. It did not matter. I accepted his generosity when it was offered. It was better that way, and I never questioned it.

CHAPTER 23

Sometimes I Had to Say No

On at least one occasion, I had to say no to a potential opportunity that came to me as a referral from another client. I was asked to contact Max Rosenberg in New York about assisting him with his real estate portfolio company and advising him on how he could improve operations and net operating profit. That was a typical request, but there was nothing typical about Max.

Although he officed in an older Park Avenue building, all of his assets were in Florida—stretching from Tampa Bay to Orlando to Jacksonville. I flew to New York for a lunch meeting, assuming that one day together would be enough to address his needs and allow me to determine if we were a good fit. Instead of meeting at the office, his right-hand man, Steve Baum, picked me up at the airport. Later, I realized Steve had his own mission—to size me up and decide whether Max could trust me. Why? Because, as I quickly discovered, the company's business practices weren't exactly on the up and up.

I had heard of three-martini lunches but had never been to lunch with someone who took that old-school type of lunch seriously. I ordered a club soda with lime and a sandwich when Max ordered his first martini. I was hungry, and this was a lunch meeting, after all. During our way-too-long meeting, Max peppered me with questions that raised some red flags, and by the time his third martini arrived, I realized what he was doing. Max was having issues with investors who had invested in property #1, a "C" property in terms of its physical condition, needing thousands of dollars for upgrades and improvements. The goal was to bring the property up to a "B" property and then sell it for a profit. Two problems existed. The property was in a "C" location, and Max had difficulty selling it even after it had been improved. He could only use funds from the next property, #2, to enhance property #1, a classic Ponzi scheme.

Before we finished lunch, I knew I would never see Max again, and I didn't.

CHAPTER 24

New York Souvenir and a Funny Surprise

On occasion, Miriam would accompany me to New York when I went there on business, but she never enjoyed spending time there. We even tried sightseeing and going to Broadway plays, but New York was just not her "thing."

Following a trip to Manhattan when I was alone for a couple of days for some meetings, I needed to get to the airport to catch an evening flight back to Chicago. When I exited the office building where my last meeting was held, I chose to walk a few blocks to get some air on a beautiful late fall afternoon when I passed by a quaint, family-run gift store. Something made me stop and look at the items for sale in the windows that faced the street. Memories of our jewelry store in Oak Park came flooding back, and I was drawn inside out of pure curiosity. I had been away on several trips and always thought of bringing something back for Miriam, but for some reason, I never did. I was always in a hurry to get to the airport and get home.

This time, however, was different. I entered the store and began looking at the New York City souvenirs. They all seemed so cheap. But then I spotted something a bit unusual: a small crystal globe with a tiny but

CUT THE TAPE EARLY!

perfect replica of Ellis Island encased within it. Maybe it was more for me than Miriam, but I hoped she would like it. All of our ancestors came through Ellis Island when they came to America, and we visited there as well. I approached the shop owner, a short, older man standing behind the counter at the register. We chatted briefly, and then I asked him how much the globe cost. Shops like this often priced merchandise to match what the owner thought the purchaser would pay. He told me, and I agreed to pay for it. As I reached into my pocket, I decided to use cash instead of a credit card. As I gave him the money, I noticed he reached under the counter to get change but never rang the register. I looked at my watch. It was 3 p.m. on the dot, and it hit me. As I smiled, he saw my expression and took the globe and the change. And then I said it. "YOU CUT THE TAPE EARLY!" He just stood there, frozen. I wished him a nice day and went on my way, laughing to myself all the way to the airport.

CHAPTER 25

An Opportunity to Work with a Developer

One of the greatest benefits of attending national real estate industry conferences—beyond earning speaking fees—was the opportunity to connect with some of the biggest movers and shakers in the business.

At a networking mixer following one of the speaking panels I participated in at a national multifamily housing conference in Orlando, Benjamin Thomas, the president of one of the country's largest multifamily development firms, approached me.

His company was expanding rapidly and had earned a reputation as a premier development, construction, and property management firm. They had transitioned from working with HUD properties to specializing in luxury housing.

When Benjamin walked up to me, he grinned as he introduced himself and shook my hand. The chemistry between us was immediately apparent, and as we began to speak, Benjamin insisted that I call him Ben. He was being shadowed by a group of people who obviously wanted time to meet with him, so I knew my time to learn about him was limited.

CUT THE TAPE EARLY!

Ben was not shy about telling me up front that his company had been growing at such a rapid pace he had lost touch with some elements of the company's operations, including the fact his bottom line had gone from making money too fast to count to a negative situation that suggested he was beginning to actually hemorrhage cash flow. I found his candid confession at a first meeting over cocktails simultaneously refreshing and concerning. My mind was already spinning with potential solutions. Still, I had learned a long time ago to slow myself down, gather information, and work toward appropriate ways to solve problems. When Ben offered to fly me down to Miami for a week to "meet his people," which included the head of each department and his controller, I accepted on the spot. We agreed that the best way forward was for me to contact his assistant when I returned to Chicago and set up a time when we both had openings on our calendars. Ben gave me his business card and again told me I had just made his day!

After I returned to Chicago, my primary goal was to set up a meeting with Ben Thomas and his key staff members. I also spent time researching his firm, looking for clues that could cause such a rapid financial collapse in what had been considered by many to be a premier company that could do no wrong. My research uncovered several potential factors behind the company's sudden change in its bottom line.

One major issue stemmed from growing resentment in Congress toward real estate developers who were capitalizing on tax laws allowing them to deduct significant sums from their tax liability legally. These laws permitted developers to structure their properties as limited partnerships, granting both general partners and limited or special limited partners favorable tax treatment.

Rather than eliminating taxes entirely, these partnerships allowed developers to defer payments—something the average profitable business couldn't do.

The end game the developers were using was to keep the properties long enough to meet the IRS tax code, thus depreciating the asset's value to the point where its value was near nothing, so when it was sold,

An Opportunity to Work with a Developer

their tax liability was also greatly reduced. In essence, if an investor or partner in a limited partnership was earning $250,000 a year, he or she could use the current IRS code to defer all or almost all of the regular income tax they would owe, so their GROSS income became their NET income.

When enough politicians in Congress learned about this from some of their jealous constituents, not only did they feel developers were abusing the tax code, but they were also not happy anyone could defer their business and personal tax liability and make more money than they were. So, they passed legislation that eliminated the loopholes in the tax code overnight, changing how businesses, owners, and investors in real estate limited partnerships could write off profits. Thus, any company owner who was not paying attention or was but felt they would be "grandfathered" into the existing tax code got caught in a very bad situation. Their entire way of structuring their properties' development, construction, and management had to recognize different ways of raising funds and adapt to other ways of operating their real estate companies.

When most successful businesses suddenly find themselves losing money, they almost always react in the same manner by trying to cut expenses first, usually starting with payroll. That is not always the best place to start turning a company around that has been earning a healthy cash flow one day and losing money the next.

Ben was eager to bring me into his company after hearing me speak at the trade conference in Orlando. During my presentation, I emphasized the importance of analyzing both sides of the financial ledger when a company faced financial trouble. In the multifamily industry, in particular, companies often overlook opportunities to generate 'other income' beyond rent. While payroll might need adjustments, every aspect of operating income and expenses—including business practices—had to be carefully scrutinized.

When I reached Ben's company in Miami a few weeks after we met, I was given a tour of the offices, met with the heads of the major operating divisions, and was given open access to meet with the people on the ground in property management. I knew from experience that while the development and construction departments sometimes had unrealistic expectations regarding how much money could reasonably be made from the operating side of the business, the property management folks usually had the best views in terms of reality and, in most cases, had already expressed concerns to the leadership. Often, their views were not heard. I quickly saw evidence that during the good times the company had enjoyed, significant funds had been provided to pay for lavish grand opening parties, which, after all, were legitimate operating marketing expenses. That said, it was cash going somewhere that could be redirected.

I completed interviews, gathered financial data, and was already writing my findings and recommendations on the airplane taking me back to Chicago. What was evident to me was not so apparent to Ben. I submitted my report along with my invoice for the services rendered. I received a short thank you in return, along with a check. The company ignored my key recommendations and moved forward as though nothing in the tax laws had changed. Unsurprisingly, they are no longer in business.

CHAPTER 26

What Do You Do When Your Client is a Putz?

I continued to attend multifamily expos and conferences around the country, both to learn and to meet potential clients in need of professional assistance. While attending such a conference in Las Vegas, I met the owner of a property management company based in Detroit but operated all their company's housing in and throughout the Sunbelt. It was the view of the owner and minority partners to follow the country's growth but acquire and manage real estate in lower-cost areas while appealing "to the masses, not the classes."

In much the same way Ben Thomas approached me in Orlando, I was introduced to the owner of Sunburst Property Management, Simon Turner when he walked up to me and told me how much he enjoyed my presentation. Simon was not as gracious or polished as Ben Thomas, but he offered me an opportunity to join him for a drink in one of the many lounges nearby to "talk."

We found a place to sit and talk for a while, with me listening while Simon spoke. He asked me questions that led me to believe he was not wholly comfortable approaching me for help. That should have been a red flag. As he continued talking, I realized my first instincts were correct and that Simon's company was in financial trouble. However, unlike Ben Thomas, Simon seemed to lack a clear understanding of leadership and how to repair the primary issues. That is why he wanted me to work with him, to tell him what, in my opinion, was "wrong" and how to fix it.

We agreed that I would go to Detroit, where I would complete a similar type of investigative analysis to the one I did for Ben Thomas in Miami. To better understand how much he was willing to share facts and data with me when I arrived, I asked for Ben's level of access when I went to Miami. Simon agreed, but I was not really sure what to expect when I got to his office in Detroit.

I decided to drive to Detroit from Chicago rather than fly and use that time to think more about how I would go about my inquiries after meeting Simon's key personnel.

When I arrived at Simon's office at 9 a.m. the next day, after getting a good night's sleep in a nearby hotel, Simon was not there at our agreed-upon time. In his absence, he had arranged for one of his senior associates to take me to the company's conference room, where bagels and coffee were available and where his key personnel began to assemble. This did not feel "right" to me, but I decided to just roll with it.

I began by introducing myself and providing a brief overview of my bio, which included my background in property management and finances and the fact that I was also a lawyer. That raised eyebrows all around the table. At that point, I became aware that Simon had not shared the reason for my visit with anyone in the company, nor had he scheduled an interview time with his key personnel. Nobody was quite sure why I was there or the financial issues within the company, not to mention where Simon was.

I proceeded to ask each senior employee to introduce themselves and set aside an hour for me that day, beginning after we had finished going around the table once. I learned they all had assignments they were working on, and this was going to be an interruption to their day.

At approximately noon, while I was interviewing key person number two, with two more to go, Simon entered that person's office and invited me to lunch. While that broke the rhythm of my interviews and planned schedule for the day, I agreed. We left in his car and drove to a nearby restaurant for lunch to give Simon an opportunity to ask me how my day was going. When I asked him why he was unavailable when I arrived and, more importantly, why none of his staff knew why I was there, he told me he had made other plans for the morning. He felt it might be better if his staff was not intimidated by him being in the office while I was there anyway.

Management styles differ from executive to executive. But this was something I did not anticipate. I could not tell if Simon's leadership style was really that hands-off or if I was missing something more substantial. We chatted briefly at lunch, but I suggested I really wanted to get back to the office so as not to lose the momentum of what I was learning and also so we did not give his key people the wrong impression about the importance of my being there.

When we returned to the office, everyone had gone to lunch. I cannot say that I blamed them, as they had no idea when we were coming back, and there was no official agenda for the day. I chose to use that time to interview Simon in his office instead, which included obtaining his views regarding his personnel, the reason he believed the company was losing money, and any thoughts he might have about how to go about making any needed changes to staff, the company's approach to how it was doing business, etc. That turned out to be a complete waste of time. Simon was vague and spoke in an unusual way that included metaphors I could not connect to my questions.

As the day went on, I interviewed the rest of the key staff, including the head of accounting. A recurring theme quickly emerged: no one truly grasped operations.

Despite being directly responsible for those areas, each senior employee I spoke with routinely deferred to Simon for answers to operational questions they couldn't address. There was no system of accountability in place—neither in writing, verbally, nor by any other means.

The company was rudderless, drifting without clear direction.

At the end of the day, I thanked each person and spent a few minutes saying goodbye to Simon. When I told him I would send my findings and an invoice for my time, he did not ask me for any hints as to what to expect. That was the strangest part of the time I had with Simon. His lack of intellectual curiosity was at the core of his company's issues. I sent my report and received a check in return. If I said this company is also no longer in business, would anyone wonder? Or care?

CHAPTER 27

Jewelry Stores, Apartments, Optometrists

What do jewelry stores, apartment properties and optometrist practices have in common? Almost nothing, but perhaps more than you realize. The core and primary function of any "front-facing" business, where employees of a company come into direct contact with customers, is – customer service. As simplistic as that sounds, it is not always seen as a core goal of many businesses.

One of the unique benefits Miriam and I derived from living in Schaumburg was the neighborhood we selected in which to reside. It was a newer subdivision where we and our neighbors all moved in about the same time. The neighborhood's makeup was quite diverse, with people from every background, ethnicity, culture, etc. In one home, directly next door, lived a married couple with two teenage daughters. The husband had worked for the same national company for years, and his wife was as friendly as though we had known her for years.

In the home directly next to us on the other side lived a younger couple who were just starting a family. A government agency employed the wife in a nearby office park, and she was able to keep regular work hours. Her husband was an optometrist who had chosen to open his own optometry practice in a less populated village about twenty miles west of Schaumburg about five years before they purchased the home next to ours. I do not remember the first person to move in; we arrived about the same time and became close friends almost immediately.

The optometrist, Doug Robinson, always had a permanent smile and a sense of humor to match. It was clear he was devoted to his wife and would make a great dad someday. Every weekend, Doug, his wife, Miriam, and I would gather in one of our backyards for a potluck dinner—followed by a kind of hootenanny.

Everyone (but me) could play a musical instrument, and many evenings, we would remain outside singing songs until past midnight. It was magical. From this bond came a request for help and an opportunity to work with Doug.

When Doug started his small optometry practice, he had the only such medical office in town. His business grew rapidly, mainly due to the fact that the residents who lived there had to travel miles to one of the larger Chicago suburbs to obtain eye exams, glasses, and contact lenses. With that, as the business grew, Doug hired more employees, and he believed he had done the right thing by going into a community that had no competition. That was, until one day, competition in the form of one of the national eye care companies arrived, offering major advertising campaigns, pricing discounts, and, in Doug's case, a reason for some of his most loyal patients to leave him.

One beautiful summer evening, I was relaxing on the deck behind our home, enjoying a beer and listening to music, when Doug wandered over from his home to join me on our deck. We chatted for a few minutes, but then I noticed something was wrong. His permanent smile had disappeared, and he seemed unusually stressed. So, I just came out and asked if something was wrong. Doug confided in me that since competition had arrived in the town where his office was, his business had been losing patients and not gaining new ones, thus putting financial pressure on his practice to the point he was beginning to believe he may have to close his optometry practice and move somewhere else.

Jewelry Stores, Apartments, Optometrists

But he had put years into building up his practice, and it was already a thirty-minute commute he did not want to make even longer. He was visibly distressed.

As Doug spoke, I just listened. I started to think back to the time I worked with my dad in our jewelry business and some marketing materials I had been reading that included the fact that the public had come to expect a higher level of service from the businesses where they spent their money. I was wondering if there was something I could do for someone who was not only a neighbor but who had become a personal friend.

I waited for the right moment and then suggested I had an idea. I offered to travel to the little town where his practice was and "check it out." At the same time, I suggested that if he and his employees would agree, I wanted to interview the staff, look at how he was marketing his practice, and try to find ways to improve operations. Doug immediately agreed. He just needed to speak to his staff and get back to me.

The following week, after receiving a "green light" from Doug, I drove to his optometry practice. I arrived an hour earlier than scheduled and drove instead through the town, paying particular attention to the storefront business, the people walking, shopping, and driving around, and then "blind shopped" his "big box" competitor. When I felt I had a baseline idea of the social-economic mix of people who lived, worked, and shopped there, and after getting a good sense of how his competition handled people coming through the door, I went to Doug's office.

The contrast was sharp and immediate. Doug had become comfortable with how his office looked to the public, how he displayed his merchandise, and how his staff approached potential patients walking into the office. I sensed he had made no effort to modernize any part of the first impression of his business since opening his doors. What stood out to me most was the meetings I had with each of his employees, including one other optometrist he employed, all of whom wore white medical coats.

CUT THE TAPE EARLY!

While visiting his competitor, I learned they offered contact lens solutions to their contact lens patients each time they updated their prescriptions following exams. I saw those same little bottles of solution for sale in Doug's office near the check-out register. This was not a CUT THE TAPE EARLY! situation. This was all about first impressions, customer perceptions regarding whether they were getting value and their money's worth from Dough's practice, and making sure Doug and each staff member knew the difference between their JOB and their FUNCTION.

After spending the rest of my day in Doug's office talking to his staff and taking photos of his merchandise materials, I said goodbye and told Doug I would be in touch in a couple of days with some recommendations. When I returned home, I went directly into my office and began to write a business plan for Doug and his business. It took several days of writing and editing to make sure I had created a basic understanding of what needed to be addressed and why. I started with the approach that included Doug gathering his entire staff for a working picnic (on a day the office was closed), which I would facilitate as soon as practicably possible. A lot had to be reviewed without delay.

The marketing plan I delivered to Doug at the end of the week began with the premise that everyone in every company, regardless of whether the company sells products or services, needs to understand the difference between their job and their function. In the case of Doug's eyecare business, I could tell he and his employees knew how to do their jobs, what they went to school to learn and deliver, and they were medically and administratively competent. But that is where their skills stopped. Not a single employee, including Doug, recognized their patients as customers, not one. This was not by design or intentional; it was an oversight. That was the first item that needed to be addressed.

Studies of human behavior show that when someone enters someone else's space, whether to buy a car, an appliance, or a physician's office, they are leaving their comfort zone. Their pulse and heart rate increase, and they can subconsciously withdraw, actually affecting their own personality behavior to become more guarded. This goes back to cave dweller days and applies to all of us. When approached in a clinical way with hackneyed, overused opening lines by an employee, such as, "How can I help you today?" it reinforces that the person being addressed is just another number, not a human being with a problem and that they entered that business to solve it.

Employees are rarely taught how to lower tension and build trust, the foundation of creating a warm, friendly environment needed for the customer to have a successful customer experience. It starts in seconds, but it can and should lead to minutes, hours, and more days of the warm customer feeling they just experienced, subconsciously making them want to work with that same person again.

That first impression is the beginning of customer retention. The patients who left Doug did so because there was no bond to keep them from going elsewhere.

I suggested Doug ditch the white coats in favor of pastel-colored polo shirts with the practice's name and logo on them. Employees were free to wear whatever color they wanted when they came to work each day without checking with anyone else. Relax the dress code!

I suggested everyone in the office relax the process of how each patient was greeted and treated. Of course, there had to be a professional medical demeanor, but each employee needed to put themselves in each patient's shoes. There needed to be a larger understanding that the same patient would likely rather be elsewhere.

As for bringing the merchandising and marketing up to current industry expectations, selling items at the check-out counter that their competition provided for free was one of the other "first things to go" that needed to change, I would ask, as would anyone, if I am paying for a bottle of lens cleaner I can get for free down the street, am I overpaying for exams, or new eyeglass frames?

The other problem Doug had was that his business practice had lost its edge in being the only game in town. They no longer held an exclusive advantage in the general community and needed to change that.

CUT THE TAPE EARLY!

I suggested Doug ask his staff for their recommendations for a personal favorite non-profit charity and vote to select one. Following that, he needed to speak to the city council to get a permit for a 5k charity run on an upcoming Saturday, and after getting approval, have several hundred shirts made in various sizes for men and women that had the name of the charity on one side, and the name of his optometry practice on the other. Finally, 100% of the entrance fee for the run would be donated to the charity, and the top three winners would also receive trophies and gift cards to several other downtown local businesses. The amount of each gift card was not as important as getting the support of the other local businesses in town that had known Doug since he opened and would continue to refer business to him. The local weekly newsletter and posters would be needed to help promote this first annual event of its kind. It was time to renew, refresh and reboot very publicly.

Doug read my findings and recommendations and proceeded to follow each and every one. We no longer live near each other, but Doug recently called to tell me to tell me the annual 5k run was still going strong, the financial bottom line at his practice bounced back stronger than before we first spoke, and he actually framed my recommendations in his home office. I love telling this story for no other reason than to point out that we all can help others if we care enough to try.

CHAPTER 28

Why I Don't Have a Business Partner

After leaving traditional employment behind and before I formed J. Roth and Associates, a former colleague asked me if I would consider assisting him with his fee management business. In multifamily property management, either the management is owner-managed or contracted out to a firm that only manages real estate for others but does not own or manage its own properties.

Gary Davis and I worked together briefly while I worked with Tony and Andy. Gary had been assigned strictly to property management functions, and while he was considered a valuable asset to the company, I always wondered how long he would stay. There were days when Gary simply did not agree with the firm's policies and procedures and gave the rest of us the impression that he was not a strong team player.

About a year before I started my own consulting company, Gary started a fee-only property management company. He came into some money from his mother's estate when she died, which was enough to get him started forming his own company. Nobody knew he had been planning to go this route for a long time, and we were even more surprised how well organized he appeared to be when, after leaving A&M

Management, he landed excellent office space in a good area and was able to assemble a team, some of whom came with him from A&M.

Despite having what Gary believed was a solid plan to create a start-up business, he got off to a slow start, and after a year of struggling to get traction, he reached out to me, suggesting we meet for a drink after work at one of his favorite watering holes. We chatted for a while about old times and then got to the reason for our meeting. His business was floundering, and he did not know what to do. He had not planned for a slow reaction from those he contacted asking for their business and was getting concerned about staying afloat. He reached out to me based on his memory of my success finding solutions to problems at our former company. He then asked directly if I wanted to join the company as a partner.

I was immediately flattered but quickly realized Gary had not thought through a potential move to bring in a partner. When I began to ask him about specifics and how well and just how bad things were for his firm financially, he avoided providing direct answers. His go-to response was to say it was not great, but it could be worse, and he knew I was the one, and the only person he could think of that would not only be a good fit for the company he started, but we could make a lot of money together working as a team.

Gary's optimism was hard to ignore, and I had always believed his knowledge of the multifamily housing industry, from an operations perspective, was solid. I needed to give his proposal some thought, so I suggested we meet again in a week, with both of us bringing our thoughts to a follow-up meeting, but next time, at his office.

When we met, I came prepared with a business plan, complete with ideas on how we may be able to grow the company and my "ask" as far as compensation if we were to become operating partners. Gary came to that meeting with nothing. No notes, nothing in writing, no plan. That should have ended our conversation, but I shared my thoughts with him anyway. Rather than focus on my ideas regarding growth, Gary was quick to put to bed any thought of forming a full partnership, suggesting instead I join the firm as an employee or consultant, with my compensation based upon hitting agreed-upon growth targets. In other words, on a commission basis, with no salary or guaranteed income to start. I was taken aback at this suggestion and not happy with his approach. When I balked, Gary explained he had to protect the cash on hand to pay bills, and he was sure we could come to a financial arrangement that would be more than satisfactory based on my ideas for growth and history of success in the business.

When Gary finished responding to my reaction to his proposal, I suggested we both needed more time to think about whether or not we should go forward and work together to save his company, and then I left. Driving back to my office, I was torn between just saying "no" and accepting the challenge if I accepted his offer.

A week later, I got back to Gary and suggested I had a plan. We agreed to another meeting, this time with me presenting an alternative compromise and a potential way for us to move forward. When we met the first time, Gary revealed the company had managed to acquire only 1,500 units under management but then hit a wall. He was able to break even at that point but still struggled to make payroll or pay other fixed expenses and another person without first adding more income from adding properties. He had suggested his goal was to remain in fee management and not give into the temptation of buying any investment real estate while running the company. Still, he wanted very much to do so at some point in the future after the company had at least 5,000 units under management.

Because Gary had marketed the company as a purely fee-based management firm, he knew that if he ever wanted to own multifamily housing, he would first have to step down from running the company.

So, he suggested he remain president and CEO of the company until it had 5,000 units under management, then move to Chairman and promote me to president and CEO. That was that carrot.

When we met the second time, I came back prepared to move forward using a fee compensation schedule that included a detailed arrangement whereby I would receive a salary that directly matched the number of units I could acquire for the company. I agreed to take the office directly next to Gary's. I was given complete and unfettered access to staff to assist me in my business plan for growing the company from 1,500 units to our mutually agreed upon 5,000 units. At that time, we were to switch offices, and I was to take over all company functions as president and CEO. We worked out some other smaller details and shook hands on it.

I never believed I could approach real estate company owners and try to replace the company managing their properties. Instead, I focused our growth on finding investors who were trying to buy properties. They needed someone to help them negotiate with brokers who represented sellers who had listed properties for sale, perform due diligence on their behalf and either recommend they buy or walk away.

Being well-known within the commercial brokerage community in the greater Chicago area, I decided to work with them first while also seeking viable investors to hire our firm to manage any properties they acquired.

I developed a strategic approach to make this arrangement mutually beneficial for both brokers and potential buyers. It was common practice for someone in my position to request a finder's fee or a commission split from a broker if I introduced a buyer who ultimately purchased one of their listings. However, I positioned myself differently—I presented myself to the brokerage community as a representative of owners and investors actively looking to expand their portfolios.

Because I was being paid directly by these owners and investors, I never asked brokers for a commission. In return for that commitment, I secured early access to properties before they officially hit the market. Of course, confidentiality agreements had to be signed, but over time, I built trust and credibility within the brokerage network. This arrangement provided me with a steady flow of investment opportunities and a critical head start in an increasingly competitive market.

To get to investors who were looking to buy properties in the area, I began working with other real estate agents who were already working with them. Many of the investors they represented worked quietly behind the scenes and did not want to be identified until necessary. These were largely investors from Canada who were very interested in buying in the United States. They were usually backed by significant family funds so they could use cash to buy and close quickly, then refinance later. That gave them an edge in a competitive market. I began working with a real estate agent who had access to a large and successful Canadian owner who perfectly fit the profile I just described. To convince that company to work with me, I offered to perform due diligence on any property they had interest in, whether they received a brokerage package from me or any other broker, quote a due diligence fee upfront before starting work on their behalf, be totally honest with my recommendations as to whether they should buy or take a pass, and finally, if they purchased the property, and gave our company the property management I would tear up the due diligence invoice. They would only be charged for my services if they passed and did not buy.

My ultimate goal was to be transparent about my recommendations. I wanted to gain the trust of any buyers I worked with and get the property managed. The fee for my time was not as important as the growth of our firm.

Building this arrangement between brokers and buyers took significant effort. At the same time, I needed to earn the trust of investors who were decisive, financially capable, and ready to move quickly—often paying cash for properties they found appealing.

That said, once I got the ball rolling, word spread fast. Both the brokerage community and investors—across the United States and Canada—recognized that our company had the expertise and infrastructure to bring buyers and sellers of multifamily properties together in a way that worked for everyone. As a bonus, it was highly profitable.

Within a relatively brief period of time, Gary's firm began to see daylight. I was getting paid accordingly, and he even had to hire more people to manage our growing real estate portfolio. As time went by, my travel to see properties picked up. I found myself working 60 to 70 hours a week, checking out real estate, meeting with more brokers and potential buyers, and preparing the due diligence reports with recommendations to buy or pass. My plan was working like clockwork, and I was giving my staff too much work to complete in a timely manner. I purchased my own computer to generate correspondence more quickly than my office assistant and to create spreadsheets for both due diligence reports and marketing materials showing how well our clients were doing with the properties we were managing. All were producing more cash flow, quarter over quarter, so I created graphs Gary and I could use to attract more fee-based business clients.

Within four years after I joined Gary's firm, we hit the magic 5,000 units under management goal. I broke out a bottle of champagne, walked into Gary's office and asked him when he would be vacating his office. He was not. He told me he was having so much fun that he had decided to revise the goal to 10,000 units. I stared at him in silence, put down my glass, packed up my office and walked out, never to return. I still do not have a partner at J. Roth and Associates and never will.

CHAPTER 29

Real Estate Syndication Firms Need Help Too

One sunny and warm afternoon, while working on filling and cleaning up my office, I received an unexpected call from a former colleague, Barry Roberts, who worked at the Owens Company. Barry was an affable and genuinely nice guy who worked hard but always had time for his family. We sometimes went to lunch together, and Barry always had at least one joke that made me laugh.

Today, his tone was different. He told me he had been following my career, had moved to New York City to accept the position of Executive Vice President of a real estate syndication firm, and had a problem he could not solve. He wanted my assistance. My first reaction puzzled me because I had been spending so much time working with real estate clients who wanted help increasing cash flow by using the creative accounting techniques I taught. I was familiar with Barry's new firm but unsure I could apply creative accounting techniques to add to their bottom line. They were a large, well-known and highly successful national firm with a reputation to match.

Real estate syndication firms, like the one where Barry was not an executive, utilized federal tax credits issued by state housing authorities

CUT THE TAPE EARLY!

across the country to develop affordable housing for individuals and families who couldn't afford market-rate rent.

In short, real estate developers—and those acquiring apartment properties—could qualify for these tax credits if they committed to setting aside anywhere from 60% to 100% of the units for tenants earning no more than 60% of the area's median income. This policy applied to new developments and acquisitions, depending on the property's location.

To avoid getting lost in the weeds here, the owners of these properties receive significant tax advantages. They can avoid investing the typical capital needed to build or buy properties that will provide them with cash flow that will be offset on their taxes by using legal write-offs and deprecation. Syndications provide the builders and buyers with funding by buying the tax credits from them and then selling them to their own investors, who are allowed to use them as tax deductions for their own companies.

The federal program Barry's firm was deeply involved with is part of the IRS Code called Section 42, more commonly known as LIHTC or the Low Income Housing Tax Credit Program. Low—and moderate-income families can afford lower rents, and both the general and limited partners make money as well. Rarely do any of these types of properties not have cash flow if managed properly because they are almost always full of waiting lists. So, why would Barry need help?

Barry briefly explained that his company had partnered with certain owners—known as General Partners—who lacked the experience or skills to keep their properties financially stable. Some attempted to self-manage, while others hired fee management companies that were supposed to have expertise in handling Section 42 properties.

To attract investors, Barry's company structured Limited Partnerships, allowing investors to purchase tax credits. This strategy enabled them to offset significant profits and legally reduce their tax liabilities.

Real Estate Syndication Firms Need Help Too

However, if any of these properties defaulted, the consequences would be catastrophic.

Like Barry's, the syndication firm would suffer in terms of their reputation, and more significantly, the investors would have a tax "recapture" issue on their hands, whereby they would owe the IRS back taxes, plus interest and penalties. For that reason, Barry's firm, when trying to solve operating problems with a partner, placed those properties on Watch Lists and assigned them to a special team in the company to correct the problem. Interestingly, the general partner (the company that did business with Barry's firm) only owned one percent of the property. In contrast, Barry's firm owned ninety-nine percent of the assets through limited partnerships (the investors), which was invisible to the public.

My conversation with Barry revealed that his company had a handful of properties in financial trouble, thus threatening its reputation. The properties continued to fail despite the efforts of several experienced asset managers in his firm to solve the issues. Asset managers typically have solid property management backgrounds and experience and act as the owner's representative for the asset in an oversight capacity.

Barry had one property in mind when calling me. A relatively small property in Wichita, Kansas, was failing despite repeated efforts to turn it around by the company's property management company, which was located in Dallas. Barry's district asset manager, regional asset manager and a senior vice president who reported directly to Barry had all tried to resolve the negative cash flow issues that could cause a default. Despite all the efforts to find and correct the problems operating at this property, it was failing. Barry was stern and direct when he asked me if I would be willing to get involved and get him and his company out of trouble with this property. I asked him to provide some background information to me before giving him my answer. I wanted the team's resumes from his company, which had failed to correct the issues, the management company's name, and the last two years of the property's financials. Barry agreed to send everything to me by overnight delivery, and I ended the call by telling him I would be in touch within a day or two after getting the request ed materials.

Barry's overnight package arrived the next day, and I dug in. I was curious why such an experienced team of professionals on Barry's team had been unable to solve the financial issues at the Wichita property. I read in the materials I received for the property in question that it had 120 townhomes with three four-bedroom units and basements, each with a detached garage. These were large family townhomes with basements and garages; the occupancy was about eighty percent, which was the big red flag that got my attention first. All 120 townhomes were one hundred percent affordable under the tax credit program, able to offer below-market rents, and from what I read, were not even trying to rent these units at the maximum allowable rent, which was baffling. I could clearly see in the latest financial reports that the property was losing money and in danger of defaulting on the deal with the lender.

I called Barry the next day and offered to work out a consulting arrangement that would pay for my time and expenses with one caveat. I wanted as much authority as possible to be able to move fast. I wanted to report directly to Barry and not involve the other members of his team who had failed to correct the problem with this property. Barry agreed to my terms; I sent him my contract for signature and then set my sights on a trip to Wichita. I created a checklist to help guide me upon arrival and started packing.

Upon arrival in Wichita the following week, I rented a car and headed for the property in question, looking for a 7-Eleven along the way where I could pick up an apartment guide. I wanted to see how this property was being marketed to the general public. I also turned on the radio to listen to some AM band stations. Both of the preceding are habits I have formed over the years when I am unfamiliar with the city I am in and where I want to learn more about the local culture.

The ad in the apartment guide was my first clue after I found the convenience store and got one. Instead of advertising the property by location (great neighborhood, near a golf course) where it should have been, it was only listed with other "subsidized" apartments. The ad said little about its features and benefits but focused on the fact it was a "low-income property with income restrictions." Neither the basements nor the garages were even in the ad. This was a colossal blunder and a red flag.

When listening to local AM band stations in the car, just about every station featured conservative commentary and religion-based programming, giving me the opinion that stereotypical "low-income housing" may not be seen by the general population as a good location to go find a place to rent. This was also a red flag in terms of how the property was being presented to the public.

When I arrived at the property, I drove through it and, using my camera, took photos of significant deferred maintenance, including peeling paint, dirt paths where the grass was missing, and decorative split rail fencing meant to add something unique to the property were broken in many locations, and on the ground. My first impression was not good. I had just passed the golf course I mentioned on the way to the property and was impressed with its pristine condition. That was another indicator that the property was not in a low-income area, per se. I believed the exterior condition would deter some from getting out of their cars and entering the leasing office.

About the leasing office, I could not find it. There was no obvious sign indicating where it was or that one of the vacant townhomes actually was an office, except for one small wood sign on the entry door. I felt myself becoming angry.

Prior to traveling to any property to inspect it and meet both the property management and on-site staff, I always called ahead and made appointments. I deliberately chose to see this property "cold" with no advance notice to the management company or staff and to shop it as a prospective tenant. When I located the office, I entered and presented myself as a possible renter. That is when things went further south.

I walked into the office and was greeted by a young man eating lunch at his desk. I said I was interested in renting a townhome. The young man asked if I had an appointment, and I responded that I did not. Then, while still eating, not getting up or introducing himself, he asked if I was employed and how much I made a year. That was his opening; how much was my income? I remained standing (guests should always be greeted by a warm, friendly person and asked to sit down in any leasing office) and asked him why he needed to know that. He proceeded to tell me the apartments were "income-restricted" and that if my income was too high, I could not live there. I had a difficult time restraining myself. This was his opening. I knew in advance the maximum allowable income I could have for a family of three or four and gave him an amount that would allow me to qualify to live there. He looked at his income reference chart and acknowledged that I could be eligible after I applied, which included paying a $75 non-refundable fee, passing a credit and background check, and bringing everyone over 18 back to the office to sign all the necessary paperwork.

At that point, I asked to see a townhome to know what to tell my wife. Unfortunately, he told me he had none he could show me. I did not understand and asked why not. He explained none of the vacant townhomes were "rent ready," and there was a company policy not to show any that weren't. I asked him, hypothetically, what if we needed to move in right away? He responded we would still need to get all the paperwork signed and pass the background test while the staff got a townhome ready for us to move into, and then we would be "all set." I suggested that was unacceptable and started to leave, expecting him to get up and do something to keep me from walking out. He went back to his lunch, and I left.

When I reached my car, I wanted to break the windows rather than use the key to unlock it. I drove to a nearby drive-thru, grabbed lunch, and then proceeded to drive to the other comparable properties in the same subject property area. I interviewed each leasing consultant or manager at the four nearest properties that would directly compete with the subject, not telling them my real reason for being there. In every case, I asked if they knew anything about the subject property, and in every case, I received negative feedback that it was a low-income property with "issues." One person told me she believed crime issues were associated with the property due to its location. This was the last nail in the coffin.

By the time I got to the hotel where I would be staying that night, I had developed a game plan in my head. After checking in, my first call was to Barry. I told him about my experience, that I would be sending photos and an initial report as soon as I could write one, and that I was planning to call the management company for the subject property in Dallas and request someone get on a commuter plane the next day and meet me at the property. I also suggested I begin looking for a local property management company with experience with Section 42 properties and arrange interviews, most likely the following week. Barry agreed to my plan and asked that I stay in touch.

My next call was to the management company in Dallas, where I was put in touch with the president and regional manager of the Wichita property. I told them I was in Wichita at the request of the limited partner and asked them to meet me there the next day. They were not happy but agreed. I wrote my initial findings, sent them to Barry, and prepared for my next meeting at the property.

When we all arrived at the townhomes, we walked the property, and then I asked to see all the vacant units without exception, regardless of condition. What I found sealed the deal for me. Rather than waste time explaining the importance of always having a vacant apartment ready to show and for someone to move into, I just ended the meeting and headed for the airport. It was clear what the next steps needed to be.

After returning to my office and settling in at my desk, I began searching for a competent property management company in Wichita. I could not understand how a property could be almost twenty percent vacant and effectively marketed and managed from a city so far away that an airplane ride would be needed to get there.

To my surprise and amazement, I was able to locate a local company in Wichita that was experienced in IRS Section 42 housing and filled with highly qualified personnel. The president of the company held a Certified Property Management (CPM) professional designation, and

CUT THE TAPE EARLY!

his company was an Accredited Management Organization (AMO), which has exacting standards for qualification. After speaking to the company's president and explaining who I represented, my role and authority, and the issues I found during my surprise visit, we agreed to meet at the property the following week. I would go to his office first and then see the property with his top regional manager and marketing director.

With the above completed, I returned to my office and requested a proposal that included a marketing and management plan. The biggest issue for the new company was how much to charge for their services and how long it may take them to get the property turned around. Typically, management fees are based on a percentage of occupancy, but that would be a losing proposition for them from the start. I agreed to a starting minimum flat fee with built-in incentives as occupancy increased. I also decided to find capital expense funding for them to spend on getting the property into a first-class condition in the shortest possible time. My goal, which they agreed to, was to have this property throwing cash flow within three months, having paid all creditors that the property owed as well. This wasn't very nice, but the property's lender and creditors were at the door. We needed to change the image of this property and clean up its reputation locally as fast as possible to survive.

I followed up with the new management company and Barry until this assignment was completed. Barry asked me to consider more assignments in the future, and I agreed to take some on, but one at a time. My experience was exhausting but extremely rewarding.

CHAPTER 30

Consulting Sometimes Means Shifting Gears

Remember the gentleman I met at the cocktail party and thought had maybe had too much to drink? Well, I did follow up as asked but never heard back from him. Then, several months later, I received a call from his assistant requesting a meeting with him.

Zachary Samuels was a gregarious, larger-than-life and well-known entrepreneur who started his career in real estate property management and, with the help of some close personal friends, created a vast empire of holdings that included apartments and just about anything that had value and could be purchased and sold for a profit. He had built a reputation as someone who literally always bought low and sold high.

But, when we finally met in Zachary's office, (he suggested I call him "Zeke," but I continued to call him Zachary, and the items he collected and stored there would require a separate chapter), he explained. At the same time, he was aware of my accounting and legal background; he needed someone smarter than anyone on this current team of experts to get a few of his largest and most financially complex assets out of the red and create cash flow. The properties were in Chicago, Detroit, and

Cleveland. Each was different, each had to be addressed as a unique entity, and each property was in the red financially.

Before accepting the assignment, I requested an opportunity to travel to each to complete my due diligence and then return with either a proposal, including the scope of work and fee schedule or let him know I would need to decline. He agreed to cover my travel and related costs, and we set a follow-up meeting for one month. My initial reaction when I visited all three assets was the amount of time and effort to reposition each, which would take time and funding, two things I was not sure Zachary wanted to hear. I prepared my proposals for each and returned a month later, at which time Zachary took less than fifteen minutes to approve them and refer me to his chief of operations to make sure I had the full support from his company that I needed.

The "Zachary special project" I accepted took on a life of its own, with me starting a checklist of what needed to be accomplished at each property to get each property to achieve positive cash flow. The more I dug into each property, the more I realized the reason his best employees had not been successful was due to the individual issues each property had. I had to visit and revisit each property more than once to wrap my head around the actual set of problems each had and not focus on the symptoms. That is where I believed the others had failed.

I had the confidence and an open checkbook from Zachary's chief of operations as I explained each step I wanted to take regarding each property. I also was very clear that it would take time to correct what was "wrong" and that I was not a miracle maker, even though I was optimistic I could solve the underlying issues at each if given enough time to do so.

Little by little, and by deferring all other potential consulting assignments on hold to focus solely on this project, I started to see progress. The Chicago property needed merchandising, marketing, and personnel adjustments that were nothing short of significant. I was met with resistance from both the on-site and regional operations staff, but the chief of operations quickly overruled them to allow me room to work. And within sixty days, we saw daylight and a trend that showed we would be throwing cash in another sixty days. That was the fastest turnaround of the three properties.

The Detroit property required capital investments and more time to get things turned around there, which took almost a year before we reached our goal. But the Cleveland property was by far the most challenging. My scope of work for this property included a repositioning that required about ten percent of what was initially invested and a three-year timeframe to get where Zachary had wanted to be. That resulted in him going back to the lender on that deal and refinancing it for $100 million more than he had initially paid, which made company history. To say the least, I was relieved, and the positive public support I received from Zachary made my time and effort worth it, as my phone began ringing off the hook when we completed that last leg of the project. Good times!

CHAPTER 31

Reaping Rewards, Taking Time Off with The Family

After achieving my primary goals, which included completing my formal education, getting a worthwhile job in an industry that interested me, finding my soulmate, starting a family, and then becoming self-employed and actually enjoying becoming successful at that, I realized, as did Miriam, we both needed a break. Miriam had the primary responsibility of raising our children, and I felt that perhaps I had not spent enough quality time with them.

Miriam, Eric, Sarah, and I sat down one weekend to discuss where each of us was, mentally, emotionally, and then we tried to determine what, if anything, should change. That was an interesting experiment that turned out to be an eye opener for me in particular.

Eric and Sarah were in their teens. Miriam had reached the point where she felt she no longer was needed as a full-time stay-at-home mom and wanted to become more actively engaged again in some form of employment. The kids were also going through their own changes, having developed closer relationships with friends I didn't even know. I felt completely out of touch and believed a seriously long (meaning more than one week), but a fun family vacation was in order. I was not sure if that meant a ski trip out west, an extended trip to a beach on either the east or west coast, or a combination of both.

I opened these ideas up to the family for discussion and was blown away at everyone's excitement at even the prospect of getting away from home for an extended period of time. So, that began my planning for a family vacation that included exactly what I mentioned above. We voted to start in a ski resort in Colorado and end up in a beach resort in Malibu. Smiles all around!

When we got home, there was enough renewed energy to light up a small city. I had gone too long before realizing the importance of just "getting away" with family.

CHAPTER 32

The Next Decade Brought Significant Changes

It has been said that time waits for no one, and there is no getting around that when life continues to move you forward like you are simply a passenger in life floating down a stream in a small boat. Over the next few years, both kids began making plans for where they each wanted to attend college. We began to lose loved ones, and after a couple of unsuccessful consulting situations, I began to wonder if my career had a "sell-by" date on it.

The friendly disagreements between Eric and Sarah about where they should each attend college made me laugh, but at the same time, I realized our "kids" were becoming adults, and their decisions could greatly influence their futures. Neither Miriam nor I wanted to interfere, but we decided to begin helping Eric and Sarah perform their due diligence regarding where to go to school, depending on their future ambitions. I wanted to reduce the apparent stress I felt was developing for them both, and at the same time, I was trying to offer some of my experience in the hopes of guiding them.

It was during this time we were hit with the sudden and unexpected death of Miriam's father, Stephen. He had a heart attack one winter day and was gone. I do not know which is worse, knowing someone is ill and being able to prepare for the eventual outcome or receiving a notification without warning a loved one has just passed away. I thought Judith handled the shock of losing her husband so suddenly with a great deal of strength and grace. Or maybe it was just a shock followed by automatic pilot. Either way, she managed to go on with her life alone, at least for now.

At about the same time, I was starting to have some difficulties getting a few clients "landed" that I thought would help us maintain a style of living we were accustomed to. My concerns became more acute when I lost three potentially lucrative opportunities in a row. I had to stop everything I was doing, take time out, and spend some time conducting my own review regarding what I was proposing. It worked.

What I had feared the most was the progression of my father's Parkinson's disease, something not covered in great detail here but was never far from my conscious mind. I knew that no two people had the same life expectancy or symptoms, but as each year passed, Dad's health was declining.

Anyone who has been a part of the "sandwich" generation will understand the additional pressures and stress of caring for and about a parent while worrying about how your children's lives will turn out. With Dad, the steps we took as his Parkinson's progressed was to help him sell that beautiful home in Oak Park and move into an assisted living community. That followed my having the "I am here to take away the keys to your car" conversation with him. While my dad and I both understood what was happening, and he knew I was doing what both Bernie and I believed was in his best interest, he did not make it any easier.

During this same time period, the kids each graduated high school with honors, made their college preferences known, applied, and were admitted. Eric had selected Northwestern University, and Sarah chose to attend the University of Chicago. Each had their own personal reasons for where they chose to go, and neither Miriam nor I felt either was making an unwise choice.

The Next Decade Brought Significant Changes

My father's health continued to deteriorate, and he required a higher level of care. Bernie and I conferred about what to do, when and how, and decided to keep him in Illinois but get him transferred into a skilled nursing facility as close to where I lived as possible, depending on the facility's ability to handle what he needed, and their rating, etc. Following his transfer, on one particular visit, Dad motioned for me to come closer so he could whisper something into my ear. "You've got to get me out of here!" he begged. When I asked why, he turned his head to look at me with a familiar impish grin and said, "Because everyone here is crazy!" As I recall, that was one of the last conversations I had with my father, and it still haunts me to this day. I imagine if he could have made it to the gift shop on his own, he would have taught the person behind the register to, well, you know, CUT THE TAPE EARLY!

CHAPTER 33

A Kaleidoscope of Memories; Sunrise, Sunset

One Sunday morning, I awoke early for no apparent reason. Then, suddenly, a wave of memories flooded my brain. Days became weeks, weeks became months, months became years, and the only explanation I had for waking that early was to address all the history that had occurred during the past couple of decades. That and the annoying, dull headache that had started to haunt me.

Miriam's mother, Judith, had been diagnosed with cancer. She was in her 80s, had managed to live independently in a modest one-bedroom apartment, and made it a point not to be a burden on either of us. But she had also been having aches and pains that seemed "out of the ordinary" and seeing doctors without telling us. The time had come for her to tell us about her diagnosis and her treatment plan and to make sure we were up to speed. The news shook both Miriam and me. Judith had been like a second mother to me, and we were remarkably close, so this news triggered unwanted memories and anxiety that I found challenging to deal with. We began to increase our visits to Cleveland to ensure we were spending important and quality time with Judith while also ensuring all "final arrangements" were in place … not my favorite thing to do.

During this same timeframe, I received notifications that friends I had attended school with (high school and college) had passed away. Naturally, this unwanted news included the fact that these were people my age or, in some cases, younger. While I appreciated the courtesy of having received them, these emails did nothing to brighten my day or make my life any more enjoyable than the one before it.

I also made sure I stayed in touch with Bernard. He had been married (the second time for both he and his lovely wife Ruth) for almost as long as Miriam and me. We talked by phone every week, and because Bernie was several years older, there was an expectation I would lose him too, someday. As my second closest friend and confidant after Miriam, I was not looking forward to that, and we chose not to discuss it.

Judith's illness accelerated quickly about a year following her diagnosis, as did our trips to see her. The end came fast, and once again, I found myself in a cemetery saying goodbye to someone I loved dearly. That was a huge loss for both Miriam and me and something I found difficult to deal with.

On a brighter note, Eric and Sarah had both graduated from college, launched their careers, and began dating more seriously—as if they instinctively knew that life's ritual included not waiting too long to take the good deals off the rack, or risk ending up in the clearance section. From graduation to working to dating, the inevitable followed.

First, Eric announced that he had met the love of his life, Paige. They had met "online" (of course) and began planning a storybook wedding. Perhaps the biggest surprise came when Eric asked me to be his Best Man at their wedding. I had not seen that coming or the joy that, as he explained, Best Man meant best friend. I will say that if no other good news ever came my way, it would not matter because that filled my heart with joy.

The wedding event came; we all danced, sang, and drank as we toasted Eric and Paige's future together. What else could anyone ask for? A grandchild on the way that is what! It did not take long for Eric and Paige to announce their family would be adding a "plus one," and we were thrilled. Henry came into the world with a smile and a promise to become a promising musician and math wizard.

Not to be left behind, Sarah had also been dating and getting more serious about one guy in particular. It was not long before she had her own announcement: She had just found the love of her life, Dylan. They had shared interests in so many areas that they both realized early in their relationship that getting married made total sense. But, unlike Eric and Paige, they chose a less formal approach that included a more intimate and lower-key wedding.

No two people are alike, and the fact we now had two happily married children was good enough for us. Eventually, Eric and Paige brought us a second bundle of joy, Jordan, who also entered the world, suggesting a life of adventure and surprises for us all.

During the same time all of the preceding occurred, Bernard hit his thirty years with the government and decided to take his pension and retire. He and Ruth had wanted to travel to Europe, and they no longer had an excuse not to go and enjoy life while they both still could. Bernie also started a small consulting business, working with clients who needed advice on how to avoid getting into trouble with the government by doing "stupid" things, like cheating on their income taxes. It was a perfect fit for Bernie, and I could not help but wonder what he would say if he had a better understanding of what I was doing with my own clients, legally, I might add, to help them also avoid paying higher taxes than legally required while using creative accounting methods to increase their net worth.

As I watched Bernard and Ruth enjoy the fruits of his labors and take trips all around Europe, I realized Miriam and I also needed to do more for ourselves. Winters "up north" were becoming more than I wanted to deal with, even though we both had grown up in cold and snowy winters. So, we joined the "snowbird" crowd and began taking winter vacations in Florida, but not back to Miami Beach, where both of our families had vacationed in the 1950s, but to the west coast of Florida. The more trips we took, the more I began thinking about where we would retire. So, on one trip to the Sunshine State, I made an effort to learn more about the various coastal communities along Florida's central west coast. I knew I had no interest in living anywhere as far south as Naples, or even Sarasota, for that matter.

I engaged the services of a real estate agent to help us find what would begin as a place to vacation but then become our permanent full-time residence when we were ready to leave Chicago. In relatively short order, we were shown and fell in love with a lovely condo in a high-rise building on Clearwater Beach. It was perfect in every way, and it did not take a lot of thought before making an offer and buying it. Thus, this became our "go-to" vacation home before we eventually moved from Chicago to Florida just a few years ago.

CHAPTER 34

You Are Hereby Summoned

Despite my best efforts to ensure that all my clients understood where to draw the line when following my advice, not everyone did. While most stayed within the lines, some crossed them or didn't know any better.

It wasn't always about greed; sometimes, it was ignorance of best practices. But either way, it was enough to attract the attention of investors—some of whom, often rightly, believed they were being ripped off.

There are several documents nobody ever wants to receive: traffic tickets, divorce papers, and being told your presence is hereby required (not requested) at a deposition where you are a key witness in a civil lawsuit. Anyone who has been deposed knows the three things they need to do before showing up:

- Hire and bring an attorney
- Remember you will be under oath, so tell the truth
- Keep your answers short and to the point.

During my entire career, either as an employee or as a self-employed consultant, I was deposed only twice, once because a client went too far with efforts not to pass along what they legally owed to their investors and then by a company that failed to accept any of my advice and did not follow best practices. In both cases, I was a self-employed consultant to the defendants and knew I was not personally in danger.

Because my consulting contract was clear about the scope of the work, there were also statements advising the client they were to make sure to keep all of their actions above the law. The language was long but clear regarding the intent, where my advice ended and where their actions were to begin. Additionally, I used indemnification language that protected me in the event they ever found themselves in legal trouble. Despite all of my actions to avoid what followed, I found myself going to depositions for a full day of grilling each time. Because I am an attorney, even though I never practiced law, I skipped the part of taking an attorney with me to either deposition. But I stuck to the script when telling the truth, kept my responses short, and let the chips fall where they may. Each deposition still took its toll on me, and that is when I also noticed the headaches were becoming worse every time I was faced with a stressful situation.

CHAPTER 35

Trying To Keep Up with Our Grandchildren!

My business life was slowing down, but it was at a perfect time. Eric and Paige had given us two beautiful and smart grandchildren who were growing up before our eyes. So quickly we had trouble keeping up with them. I do not want to even guess how many photographs and videos I have from grade school, middle school, and then high school. Both Henry and Jordan were excellent students and fully engaged in extracurricular activities.

Despite the pressures of keeping up with business obligations and trying to find relief from my headaches, I never lost sight of the fact that watching our grandchildren grow up had a limited window of time. I had already missed some of Eric and Sarah's birthdays, along with other major events, because I had let business take priority. I didn't want to make that mistake again.

Eric and Paige had moved to Atlanta, while Sarah and Dylan settled in Phoenix—each pursuing their own dreams and careers. For the most part, seeing them meant that Miriam and I had to travel to visit—not just them but also Henry and Jordan.

I had so many frequent flyer miles, as well as hotel and car rental points, that money for travel was not an issue. Besides, we had been successful enough financially, between my business income and investments, to not let money (or the lack of it) get in the way of staying personally in touch with our children and their families.

Before we knew it, both Henry and Jordan were looking at colleges around the country. Boy, did that bring back memories. Where did the time go? Miriam and I both realized we had fewer days ahead of us than behind us and were determined to make staying in touch with our family a higher priority. I also wanted to reduce some of my business travel and convinced everyone to get to Florida to visit us there each winter so we all at least knew we would be seeing each other no less than once a year, no matter what. That became our new focus.

CHAPTER 36

When A Close Friend Needs Help

One of the perks of being self-employed is the ability to establish your own schedule and, from time to time, make an effort to see friends from the past, both from college and high school. As I continued to push forward with my consulting business, I found myself looking back at my past more often and remembering the more memorable people I knew and special events that I could easily associate with them. I had been slowing down myself, dealing with some aches and pains, taking more time off, and still dealing with headaches that were becoming more frequent and becoming more painful. Perhaps I needed to spend even more time seeking out old friends from my past and better diversify my time.

One such friend who came to mind often but whom I had neglected to reach out to was Sandra Berman. Sandra and I have known each other since third grade and grew up about a street apart from each other. Once in high school, we became even closer friends. She did not have a brother, and I did not have a sister. There were other things that brought us closer together in high school. She wanted to date a guy her parents would not be happy with, and I wanted to date a girl my dad would not approve of. In our senior year, and as prom was getting closer, we each laughed about what our parents would do if we went to prom with the people we wanted to go with anyway. This subject came up one day as we walked home after school (there were no buses). When we reached the street where we typically parted ways to get to our respective homes, we stopped and continued talking about what we each wanted but could not do. At the same time, I asked Sandra if she was going alone to the prom or staying home. When she hesitated, I just said, "You are going, but not alone. We are going together!"

She broke out in laughter and then teared up and said, "Only you would propose something so outrageous!" But I was serious. I did not think we should both be penalized for attending one of the biggest events of our high school experience. So, we made it official. She bought a new dress, I got a tux, and we found transportation to go to prom as a couple. We had a blast and cemented a life-long friendship that still exists to this day.

Memories of prom had me thinking about Sandra—and wondering how her little cat house was doing. Oh yeah, the cat house. The running joke was that after college, Sandra moved to California to teach, living with one of her sisters. But one day, she realized she wasn't happy and decided to move back to Chicago. With a mix of savings and courage, she set out to find a storefront near where we both grew up—opening a retail shop devoted to food, toys, and other essentials for cats and their owners.

Dogs were a part of her business plan, but the vacant store she found was small and located in Cicero, so it became Cicero Cats. She neither sold nor boarded cats; she just purchased and then re-sold items of interest to cat owners, hopefully for a profit.

One day, I was driving through Cicero on my way to look at some real estate for a friend and decided to drop in unannounced to see my friend Sandra. She had been in business for more than fifteen years, and I was sure she would enjoy lunch out with me. I parked near her store and walked in. What I saw astounded me. The store was smaller than I expected and packed with merchandise everywhere. Cluttered would be a more accurate description. I called out to Sandra because I did not see anyone in the store. When she appeared from the back of the store carrying a bag of cat food, she stopped, dropped the bag, and ran to me, giving me a tight hug, which lasted long enough for me to need air. She was shocked to see me after not having seen each other for such a long time and was just taken aback. I suggested we get lunch, but she declined, saying she could not leave the store unattended. She had no help and certainly could not lock up in the middle of the day.

Without probing further why she could not leave, I suggested I go down the street, get some take-out and bring it back for both of us. She agreed. Over lunch in her store, a few customers came and went, and she was selling merchandise, so I began to ask how she was doing. After a brief silence, she told me she was on the verge of going broke. And she was depressed. Her car was 10 years old; she had spent years trying to make enough money to retire and was only breaking even. I was both astonished and heartbroken. I decided to come back when I had more time and have a longer conversation about trying to help change that, so we said goodbye, and I left.

Before I returned to see Sandra, I prepared a list of questions about the financial part of her business, how she handled inventory, kept track of both purchases and sales and created talking points about how she could change her business model if my suspicions were correct. I called to set up an actual working appointment after normal working hours but in private. Again, I would bring take-out dinner for us both. Sandra agreed to meet but sounded skeptical about what we could accomplish. I just told her I had some thoughts about her business and wanted to share them.

Prior to heading out to meet with Sandra, I purchased a small metal lock box and a couple of ordinary accounting ledgers sold in an office supply store to take to our meeting. Once at her store, we ate, and I just started asking questions about what she felt she had done right. But also, what went wrong. In that conversation, I noticed a small sign near the cash register that read, "Five percent Discount for Cash Purchases." Sandra had started to take credit cards about two years ago, as they were becoming more popular. These were the early days for people using credit instead of cash, but the retailer had to pay the bank a fee for their use. Sandra's profit margin was so small she decided to encourage cash sales but continued to take credit cards and pay the banks for those transactions.

Suddenly, I had an idea about how to present where I believed our conversation was going to go anyway. I asked her if she remembered her dad's and uncle's butcher shop in one of the other Chicago suburbs that had closed several years ago. She certainly did. And did they take credit cards? Of course not; everyone paid for everything with cash. Then I asked her how she believed she and her two sisters got to go to college; more specifically, who paid for that? She sat there looking at me and said, "My dad." I just smiled, got up, and walked to the front counter, where I took down the sign and then placed the metal lock box under the counter. We then spent a few hours discussing real life, like when you are the owner of a small business that takes only cash, and how people like her father kept track of what he paid for beef and how much he sold it for. More importantly, how some of the cash from sales started to go under the counter at some point each day, which eventually paid for college, vacations, new cars, etc. Sandra sat there in silence, so I told her about Roth Jewelers, and then it just came out. Sandra, if you want to retire someday, you are going to have to CUT THE TAPE EARLY!

So, there it was again. And at that point, Sandra and I began a conversation about her concerns that she would be committing a crime by not paying taxes on income if she took my advice. We talked at length about how many more people than she could ever imagine who ran small family businesses could survive, send their kids to college, give money to charity, take vacations, and … retire. Our conversation dragged on, and it was getting late. I suggested she give what we had been discussing some serious thought and call me so we could meet again.

Two weeks passed before I heard from Sandra. She invited me to return to the store again but would not say why. When I arrived, I found a vastly different, neat, tidy store. Inventory was displayed much differently; some items were marked down "on sale," and I noticed the prices on some of her cat food and other best-selling merchandise had been increased. As I strolled through the store, I looked back at Sandra, smiling and pointing to a new sign near the cash register that said, "CASH ONLY PLEASE." I was stunned. I asked Sandra if she was still accepting any credit cards. She said a few customers insisted on paying for what they bought with a credit card, but they agreed to pay five percent extra for the privilege. Those sales went into a ledger with other cash sales, but there was a label on that book that said AM. I noticed, under the counter, a second book labeled PM. She had heard me and had made a conscious decision to change direction, get out of her safe but failing routine, and be happy supplying long-time customers with good products, good service, and an attitude to match.

So, what made her change her mind? "You did," was her short response. "You have always been the one person I could trust to look out for me and who cared." Sandra's eyes welled up with tears. I got another hug, and then she pulled out a travel brochure for Florida. She was making plans to take a vacation! I left the store a bit light on my feet. I felt in my heart that all would be well for Sandra, and I smiled.

PART 5

WHAT'S NEXT?

CHAPTER 37

Looking Back, Looking Forward

On a late afternoon winter day while vacationing with Miriam at our Clearwater Beach condo, I blurted out, "Let's just stay here." The sun was slowly sinking toward the Gulf of Mexico; it was warm but not hot, and a nice breeze was blowing toward the beach. Miriam had been reading a book but turned and looked at me with a bit of a smile on her face.

"Are you serious?" she asked.

I did not respond immediately. My mind had become a black-and-white movie reel, going back to my early days, from growing up in a loving family environment to losing my mother at just thirteen, attending school, then working with my dad, and all the great experiences I had when I began a career that had taken me for quite a ride. We were blessed to have such great kids, grandchildren, friends, and extended family. I had probably reached the point when I didn't know if I wanted to continue working.

During the past few years, I have made a stronger effort to take more time off to spend with my one real hobby, photography. But my mind never really shut down, and I never mastered the art of complete relaxation. Miriam and I had talked about retirement, but neither of us felt comfortable in actually planning for it. To keep busy and do the things that interested her, Miriam had started several different businesses over the years to stay busy, but more than anything else, besides finding ways to volunteer and spending time with our family, gave her the most joy.

She could also read for pleasure for hours at a time without putting an enjoyable book down, something I had not mastered. My reading material was almost always connected in some way to my work. When my headaches progressed to the point where I sought medical advice, I also began to lose interest in taking every call and responding to every email asking for assistance with a problem some business could not solve. My desire to continue traveling for clients had reached the point where just planning that trip, any trip other than to come down to our condo in Florida, was not something I looked forward to anymore.

The sun continued to drop lower in the sky, painting its vibrant and soft colors as it moved toward its eventual meeting at the water. I left the balcony and went inside to get my camera to get just one more photo of the perfect sunset. I had taken over a hundred sunset photos from our balcony. Still, none had ever met my own personal standard of "perfect," meaning that moment when the sun kissed the water as it continued to sink, leaving a brilliant palate of colors that turned the sky into a piece of art. Maybe, just maybe, this would be the "one." I aimed, held my breath, and fired. The shutter accommodated my request, and I had one more photo that was likely suitable for framing. I would need to see it on my computer and make sure I had what I wanted. Some of my friends used to tell me I was too much of a perfectionist. To counter what I considered an unflattering comment, I would always tell them, "No, I was a precisionist." And they just did not know or understand the difference. Neither did I, quite frankly, but I usually had the last say.

Miriam brought me back to the present with a suggestion: we go to one of our favorite casual dinner haunts to grab a bite to eat and relax. That was a good idea and one that Miriam instinctively knew would be a good way and place for us to have a conversation we had both been avoiding. After we were seated and ordered, and each had a sip of wine, I found Miriam just looking at me with a quizzical look on her face. I knew she wanted me to tell her what was on my mind. Having a more formal but quiet place to talk made that easier. I asked her what she wanted to do and what WE should do. But Miriam did not respond. I sensed I was being asked to suggest a plan we could both live with. So, as our dinner arrived, I just said it. "It is time to sell the house in Schaumburg and move to Florida as a permanent resident." As if God himself overheard me, there was a clap of thunder, followed by a sudden cloudburst outside the restaurant. These can be common events in Florida. They last only minutes, then it stops, and the sun comes back out, at least in the daytime.

We sat and spoke for a couple of hours, just throwing around ideas about timing, logistics, and asking ourselves if this was the right time to make this move. By the time we left the restaurant, we had a plan. It was now time to call the kids and share it.

During the following weeks and months, we were able to find a buyer for our Schaumburg home and finalize the move to our Clearwater Beach condo. After settling in, Miriam and I each took some well-deserved time off, catching up on personal things we both needed to do and enjoying a mental break from many years of nonstop work.

As time stretched from days into weeks and months, I began to miss the days when someone would reach out to me and ask for my help with a project. Little by little, I began to accept consulting assignments again, but this was tempered by my desire for a more balanced lifestyle and the fact I was now being seen by more than one physician to find out why the headaches that had plagued me for so long would not go away.

I have had a lot of quality time to think about what I did as an adult, what I would do differently if I could go back in time, and what I actually felt good about. At the end of the day, although there were a few regrets, I had achieved a great deal for an average kid who grew up during a time when anything happening in the world could have altered my thinking. Not wanting to retire completely drove my decision to return to the real estate business, but this time only as a realtor.

Looking back, there was one true constant in my life—one rock, one defining presence that always stayed with me: the time I spent with

CUT THE TAPE EARLY!

my father after my mother's untimely passing. Beyond having a brother I could always count on, I remained deeply aware of how fortunate I was to have that time with the one person who undoubtedly shaped me more than anyone else. My dad was never my mind—his influence was, and always will be, a guiding force in my life. So, while I am still working on creating a better balance between the work I continue to do and the additional time I now have to spend with my family, I always remember each day to stop what I am doing at about 3 p.m. and spend a few quiet moments focused on the most important lesson in my life. CUT THE TAPE EARLY so I can reap the harvest of my efforts and hard work. How else would I be able to relax on the balcony of my condo, overlooking what some never get to see? Thanks, Dad; I love and miss you, but most importantly, I always feel you are with me.

About the author

Jerry R. Rosen is an executive with a track record of performance and excellence in the real estate industry. His expertise covers the full range of acquisition analysis, marketing, property and asset management of residential investment-grade real estate, covering 40 years of experience throughout the United States. Mr. Rosen has supervised managing more than 50,000 multifamily units in 40 States, plus the District of Columbia and Puerto Rico. He directed the initial staffing, marketing, and successful stabilization of more than three dozen multifamily properties, supervised the activities of more than 1,000 personnel, performed due diligence assignments for the acquisition, new development, financing or refinancing of more than 100 properties, and directed the successful repositioning of more than two dozen non-performing or under-performing real estate assets. In addition to his professional achievements, he has been a member of the Elyria, Ohio Jaycees as well as the president of the San Mateo, California Jaycees, and served as a Guardian Ad Litem in the Circuit Court of the Thirteenth Circuit, State of Florida, County Juvenile Division.

When Mr. Rosen became self-employed in 2005, he read, Find your IT[3] and then do it to help others. My mission is to help people achieve their goals by providing them with the knowledge and the tools they need." Mr. Rosen has stayed busy operating Investment Real Estate Advisors, a real estate consulting business, JR Rosen Consulting, assisting start-up and small business owners to grow and improve operations. In 2006, he became a licensed real estate agent in the state of Florida, often working with only one or two clients at a time, sometimes pro-bono, to ensure his clients could achieve a lifelong dream of their own. Despite staying busy every day with work-related projects during his 'golden years," Mr. Rosen also manages to find time to devote to his wife of more than 50 years, their children and grandchildren. His hobbies include travel and photography, often combining the two.

Note: Mr. Rosen has included information in Cut The Tape Early! based on true accounts, changing some details to avoid revealing the true identities of the individuals he has portrayed.

---

[3] Smart, J. Alfred. Find Your IT!

www.ingramcontent.com/pod-product-compliance
Lightning Source LLC
Chambersburg PA
CBHW052145070526
44585CB00017B/1980